CHRONICLES OF 20TH CENTURY BARBADOS: VOLUME 1

Identities

Book One

ELOMBE (Elton Deighton Mottley)

FAT PORK
10-10
PRODUCTIONS

Second Edition. First Published in 2003.

**FAT PORK
10-10**
PRODUCTIONS

Fatpork Ten-Ten Productions
PO Box 12, 9 Gordon Town, Kingston, Jamaica
elombe@cwjamaica.com

Edited by Carol A. Pitt and Yejide Maynard

ISBN 978-149-7317-87-1 (paperback)

These essays were first published in the
Nation Newspaper, Fontabelle, Bridgetown, Barbados

*For my children Deighton, Adunni,
Akintunde, Oluyomi and Jaja*

and

my wife, Donna Marie

Table of Contents

Foreword

In his two-volume collection, Identities, Elombe has created a mirror for Barbados equalled only by the likes of George Lamming, Kamau Brathwaite, Timothy Callender and Austin Tom Clarke. In this collection of short essays he takes us on a journey of life; his life, and ultimately the lives of people who have influenced him most—Bajan people. Whether he is speaking about a tuk band man he knew when he was a boy or being a student at the University of Manitoba in the 1950s, Elombe's insights reflect the sharpness of a good social scientist and the sensibility of an artist. Elombe is essentially a humanist who has strong views about the location of Caribbean people in the wider world. Implicit in his work is the belief that, like other Caribbean people, Barbadians have a unique civilization which is largely the result of its African heritage. Elombe leaves no doubt where he stands with regard to his country and the Caribbean; he is a nationalist, a regionalist and Pan-Africanist.

While his writing is clear and forthright, there are times when he writes like a poet, playing with metaphors—not simply words, but also situations. Whichever style is adopted, he is always provocative.

Identities takes us where no man or woman has gone before, with regard to the discourse on society in Barbados. This is both a conversation with and about Barbados; about its history, culture, strengths, weaknesses and prospects. Elombe's essays are parsimonious, but these concise and skilfully crafted essays open up a window to Barbados and Bajans with immense clarity and rigour, and in a way hitherto unseen. Moving between the subjective and objective, the idiographic and nomethetic, these essays reveal a picture of Barbados from within and without, without being too pedantic or didactic.

The range of subject matter is also amazing. Some of his essays are meaningful epitaphs to a side of Barbados that has long disappeared with the rise of modernism. Others are about issues which never seem to disappear from the landscape of Caribbean society: issues such as race and social justice, recognition, nationalism, self-esteem, technology, development, to mention a few. In volume I he is more concerned with issues of culture and identity construction. In volume II he places greater emphasis on issues of social and economic justice, race and development. Elombe's texts (and subtext) pose (though not always answer) a number of important questions for Barbadians. Questions such as: Who are we? Why are we the way we are? What is our contribution to world civilization? What are some of our failures? What are some of our strengths? What can we do to make Barbados a stronger and more prosperous place?

Obviously, in collections of this type, different themes tend to resonate with different people. As a sociologist I am immediately struck by his numerous discussions on race and stratification in Barbados. To understand Barbados' social structure, one has to understand its history. And while the country has much in common with its Caribbean neighbours, there are also important differences. In one of his pieces Elombe puts his finger on one of the unique features of Barbados, when compared to the other Caribbean islands. He points out that

> "[T]he presence of the plantation house in Barbados is unlike any in the Caribbean. This is so in respect to the number, the size and the architecture. The owners of these great houses were residents in Barbados and therefore all

of their wealth was in Barbados. They were not absentee landlords like those found in the other islands."

Although well known by historians, it is a point often lost on many students of Caribbean studies who seek various explanations for what they see as Barbadian exceptionalism. More important though, for Elombe, in that same article, is that most of the wealthy whites in the Barbados are not the descendents of that early planter class. Instead these are descendents of the poor whites who also suffered at the hands of the early planters and the British during slavery. Thus Elombe is understandably surprised that such a group is not more understanding of the concerns of black Barbadians regarding troubling aspects of the country's history. Elombe leaves us in no doubt that the problem of race and inequality in Barbados is a work in progress and needs to be confronted more honestly and openly than has been in the past.

On a different note, Elombe uses these pages to remind Barbadians of their past. Combining the skills of a teacher and an entertainer, he is able to do this by drawing on his personal experiences, and bringing to life events and people he speaks about. In one essay he focuses on the famous (or infamous) Harry's Nitery, which was a Bridgetown institution. He is able to show us how that nightclub reflected a liberal side of Barbados and embraced global culture, at a time when the country was attempting to shake off the political and cultural shackles of mother England.

Elombe is especially compelling in his accounts of ordinary Barbadians who are the backbone of the society. Whether in his stories of Reginald Barrow, Rupert Yarde and Professor Laha (who, like Elombe, was the first magician I ever met) or the "sweet, sweet" music of the tuk band man, he brings a fresh and authentic voice to the discussion of people who often slip between the cracks of the history books. Elombe discusses the impact that these ordinary men made on his life. By exposing these personal accounts, he is able to recapture a bygone era, giving meaning to the work of these people in the context of nation building and cultural evolution. Also, by putting a face on the activities of these ordinary people, the reader is treated to people who carry themselves with dignity and a sense of purpose. These people are placed before us in a way which forces Barbadians to confront their/our mirror image.

Elombe's passion is evident in his discussion of music, especially calypso and jazz. But he also demonstrates a rare breadth and depth in his pieces on the music of other countries and regions. This passion is also evident in his writing style, moving between British and American English, and Bajan. He does this with a level of confidence and ease, typical of a person who is comfortable in his skin. While his style also reflects his obvious mastery of English (Elombe was schooled in the classics at one of region's leading educational institutions, Harrison College) and his native Bajan, he seems more interested in communicating with his audience. He understands that language should not become a fetish. That it is an instrument of expression and its usefulness is largely determined by the extent to which it is able to communicate ideas. Thus at times he opts for the sheer simplicity, but effectiveness, of a Bajan expression over English.

Elombe's tone is always conversational. Witness for example an extract from his piece 'Bull Cow and Chicken':

"When bull cow was small, he had a vision. He look up in de sky one night and he see de dipper. I ent kno if it was de Big Dipper or de Lil Dipper or if it did a Dipper at all, but next ting yuh kno, bull cow decide he ent eating nuh more cane meat."

This is a powerful statement about struggle and change, and written in a way that has strong resonance with his Barbadian audience.

Identities is an outstanding work by one the Caribbean's brightest sons. The pieces were originally written to communicate with a mass audience, but they should also be important additions to the reading lists of scholars of Caribbean society. There is a strong theme of continuity and change running through the book. Students and teachers of Caribbean Studies and Cultural studies should make sure that they have this gem in their possession.

Ian Boxill, PhD
Senior Lecturer in Sociology
University of the West Indies
Mona, Jamaica

Acknowledgements

First I must thank my wife Donna who encouraged me to start writing this weekly column for the Nation in Barbados. Secondly, she was also the first to read my articles and her editorial comments helped me to clarify some of the issues that I raised in these articles.

I am also grateful for all of those Bajans who throughout the years assisted me by answering my questions or pointing me in the right direction. Whether I praise them or criticize them, they are part of the panoply that helped me in my search to identify us as Bajans or Caribbean people. I am also very thankful to have met most of them and can say that some residue of those meetings have remained with me.

I would also like to thank the Nation and its staff who helped in one way or another: Harold Hoyte. Roxanne Gibbs, Roy Morris, Harry Mayers, Chris Gollop, Errol Niles and all the members of the editorial staff who from time to time provided me with critical information.

My thanks to Elaine Melbourne for taking time to read these essays and for offering very valuable suggestions. To Ian Boxill also goes my thanks for his comments and for consenting to write the foreword.

My thanks also go to Debbie Stoute Lynch and Denise Gooden for proofreading the manuscripts, to Carol Pitt and Jide Maynard for editing, and to Caribbean Chapters Publishing for the layout and design. Any errors of judgment, reasoning or accuracy are mine.

Image Credits

The photographs used in these books were either sourced from my private archives, the Mottley family archives, or were published by the Barbados Government Information Service (BGIS), the *Barbados Advocate*, the *Barbados Annual Review*, the *Barbados Daily News*, the *Nation News*, the *Sunday Sun*, the *Beacon*, the Caribbean Broadcasting Corporation (CBC), the *Trinidad Guardian*, the *Trinidad Express*, the *Jamaica Gleaner*, or from various sources on the Internet. The names of many of the photographers who worked for these media houses never appeared on the photos, but the author acknowledges their work in documenting the history of Barbados. The following is a partial list of some of the photographers.

Art Tappin
Cecil Marshall
Charles Grant
Cyprian LaTouche
Dada Brewster
Darnley Bushel
Erad Brewster
Errol Nurse
Fitzpatrick
Frank Grimes
Frank Lashley
Gordon Brooks Jr
Gordon Brooks Snr
Junior LaTouche
Livy Grimes

Maurice Giles
Mike Williams
O'Neal Oliver
Parkinson
Paul Mandeville
Perce Tappin
Richard Barnett
Ronnie Carrington
Roy Byer
Seth Skeete
Tumpa Greaves
Val Millington
Vondel Nichols
Willie Alleyne
Willie Kerr

While every effort has been made to trace the owners of other copyrighted material reproduced herein, the publishers hereby apologize for any omissions and would be pleased to incorporate missing acknowledgements in any future editions.

Introduction

I WROTE these essays for the *Nation* in Barbados between
1997 and 2000. I called the column *Identities* because it was
through a multiplicity of individuals—ancestors, elders and
contemporaries, that I began getting answers to the questions I
had been asking myself as a boy. Who am I? Who or what is a
Bajan? Who or what is a West Indian? What makes me different?
Why are some of us black and why are some of us white? Why
are we treated differently? Why do I respond to certain music
which I was told was bad? I am not sure I have answered these
questions, but I certainly wanted to share the search with you.

I was born on May 5, 1938, just before World War II started. I
was conscious that school books never spoke about me—about
us. Except for the occ-asional *Ebony* and *Sepia* from the United
States of America, I never saw us, black people, written about
in books. Sometimes we appeared in the newspaper, mostly
cricketers or politicians.

The first time I read about black people was in a book my
father brought home from the House of Assembly Library. It was
Melville Herskovits' *Trinidad Village*, which I read when I was
sixteen. He brought other books which I also read: Raymond
Smith's *The Negro Family in British Guiana*, J. A. Rogers' *From
Superman to Man*, and George Lamming's *In the Castle of My Skin*.
He also brought two women to our house—one white and one
black. The white woman was Connie Sutton, an anthropologist
(later a Professor at New York University), who was studying

the community of Ellerton, St. George. The black woman was Paule Marshall, an aspiring novelist, who was researching her family history in St. Andrew. I was impressed that they thought ordinary people in Barbados were important.

Barbados was a world where change was very slow, so that many of the people who were born before me, my ancestors and the elders, shared almost the same world for generations. The knowledge they shared is almost always prefaced by "I kno you befo yuh born!" Or they could recall somebody in 'yuh family', or an incident that I had heard before. These stories always gave me a reference point to understand Barbados.

My world started its rapid change in the late fifties when I went away to study. But this only intensified my desire to know more about Barbados. When I returned shortly before Independence, this desire led me into every village in Barbados talking to people, recording their stories and their thoughts, their voices and their songs. *Identities* kept changing and shifting, yet beneath the surface things remained similar and constant. Many of these stories will be annotated in other books. Others are from my own experiences, which to me illustrate the continuum in which I live and which continues to influence my outlook on life.

For those of you who have never read some or all of these stories before, these two volumes will give you an idea of the richness of Barbadian and West Indian culture. The people in them are real and fascinating and I enjoyed many, many hours sitting at their feet learning from their wisdom or observing their behaviour.

For now, ah gone!

Elombe
elombe@cwjamaica.com

The Bearded Fig Tree

The Bearded Fig Tree

GETTING TO Batts Rock Beach was not a problem if yuh walking. Yuh could come from Brandon's along Brighton Beach, pass Paradise and yuh dey. Or you could come down de road by the Lazaretto. This road however was an adventure for a car— big rocks galore, like precipices and holes big enough to hold a jacuzzi.

Batts Rock Beach was best known as a Sunday morning cricket beach. Tucked round de corner from the Point, it was hemmed in by the cliffs and the sea on the North. But on the East, it was dominated by a magnificent Bearded Fig Tree.

The Bearded Fig Tree—the name that legend suggests was the origin of the name Barbados; indeed a magnificent tree, its huge branches spreading like the giant umbrella of an Ashanti Chief. Its prodigious roots like the locks of a Rastaman descended earthwards and colonizing the coralstone cliffs with an army of siblings all ready to do duty in case a hurricane blows by.

The Bearded Fig Tree—the name of a night club nestled in the rock crevices, behind the fortifications of the rock-steady roots. Perfection in seclusion with only the stars and the visiting moon as witnesses to the nefarious carryings-on.

It was a scene from a Hollywood B movie starring the likes of a Humphrey Bogart or a John Garfield or a Dane Clark, the hard-nosed adventurer, a rapacious consumer of raw whiskey or green rum, who is on the rebound from a two-timing wife or some disastrous affair. Or maybe he is a retired secret service agent mortified by further intrigue or tired of the incessant tensions of the job.

He is usually found on some island in the Caribbean operating a leaky old fishing boat or living on a beach in a grass hut and sleeping in a hammock or running a beach bar for some other seedy expatriates like himself.

And hanging around providing comfort, food and protection, is the native woman. In Hollywood style a half-caste good-hearted prostitute, but in reality a black woman who sees the possibility of improving her lot.

Whatever the screenplay was, the Bearded Fig Tree was actually run by a mysterious expatriate who, enamoured by the Bearded Fig Tree and its legend, created on this hillside in the late fifties early sixties the night club, The Bearded Fig Tree. And his woman was black, a good cook and no doubt an even better companion for the backroom that served as their home.

The Bearded Fig Tree became the hang-out for expats and average Bajans. It wasn't like Club Morgan or Coconut Tree Club with its clientele of Gold Coast residents and their guests. It didn't feature a formal Cabaret like the others, but a heavy dose of real calypso.

Lord Radio was the resident calypsonian. Oliver Broome is his real name. He took the name of Lord Radio after King Radio (Norman Span), one of Trinidad's most outstanding calypsonians of the 1930s. And they do look alike.

I met many calypsonians there. It was Radio who introduced me to the Mighty Dougla, who had just defeated Sparrow for the monarchy in Trinidad. Sparrow was livid and felt it

LORD RADIO

was robbery, but V. Dougla, half-African half-East Indian, was a humble conqueror.

But still the Bearded Fig Tree and the legend of the naming of Barbados makes little sense. Especially since these trees are found in most of the islands of the Eastern Caribbean.

The same reason that people called Wavell Avenue 'Jack-Muh-Nanny Gap' is the same reason that European sailors and adventurers would call the island 'Land of the Bearded Men'. Both names reflected reality. There were bearded men on Barbados.

The significance of this is noted in the fact that Arawaks and Caribs genetically produce no facial hair in the form of beards. The implication of this is that the Amerindians would have had to mix with another people who genetically produce facial hair. Such people could only have been Africans, who were frequent travellers to the Caribbean long before Columbus.

Just as Dougla reflected the mixture of his African/East Indian heritage in his prize-winning calypso *Split Me in Two*, the Bearded Fig Tree, with its dangling roots searching for an anchor, symbolizes our search as a people for a sense of rootedness.

From this first interaction between Africans and American Indians, the Caribbean has been defining itself in new terms. The master/slave relationships of Europeans and Africans (in spite of the slave laws) produced new definitions—mulatto, quadroon and octoroon. The African/East Indian mixture has produced the term douglah. I have never heard a name for the substantial interrelationships between Chinese, Africans, Indians, Europeans and Assyrian/Lebanese. The absence of names in no way negates the existence of such relationships.

What is happening in Guyana and Trinidad and Tobago is totally unnecessary. Maybe we need a new legend for the Bearded Fig Tree.

Pressures on Being Black

EAGLE HALL was my stomping ground and the Roxy Theatre my mecca. And whatever the memories were of white images on that silver screen, I decided to hold a Miss Eagle Hall contest for black girls on the stage of the Roxy theatre.

It was 1970. Black was beautiful. Black Power was helping us to redefine ourselves in a very hostile environment. Many of us renamed ourselves and asserted our Africanity. We sang praises like griots of long forgotten ancestors. We learned the meanings of admonitions like "yuh don't sweep yuh house after dark" which meant that sweeping out a house after dark would bring bad luck because you may sweep out the good spirits and leave the bad ones. In African tradition, it is accepted that the spirits come into the house at nightfall.

And Errol Barrow passed the *Public Order Act* for Bobby Clarke and myself to stop the meetings and the talk. When it was thought that I might have been a candidate in the 1971 elections, my voice and features were banned from CBC radio and TV. But this in no way stopped the talk. Tom Adams promised to repeal the Act when the BLP won. He never did,

BOBBY CLARKE

ERROL BARROW

8

and it has never been repealed.

But the issues were important, real, and relevant. Four years after independence, black people were still marginalized in a society that we helped to build from the bottom up. Generations of us suffered the indignities of being treated worse than animals, and valued less at that. We had no names except those the slave master on whose plantations we were born gave us.

We could not object when our women, our mothers and our sisters were raped and seduced by that same slave master. (In a genetic study done in the USA, over 70 percent of blacks were said to carry European genes. I wonder what it would be for Barbados.) We endured bouts of depression when we were taken from our mothers and sold to other plantations. Our mothers suffered most of all knowing every time they had children, they would be taken from them without warning.

So in the sixties, few blacks were working in Barclays, Royal Bank, CIBC, or Nova Scotia. Black people seldom were used in ads on television or in newspapers. No blacks managed or were in any managerial positions in most if not all of the stores on Broad Street. The same obtained at Barbados Light and Power, the Telephone Company and Cable and Wireless. The Mutual, Barbados Shipping and Trading, Manning's, Da Costa's, A.S. Bryden's, Plantations Limited (except for Lisle Ward and that was due to his father's traditional proclivity, which he acknowledged), McEnearney Garage, Courtesy Garage, Fort Royal, and KR Hunte were closed to blacks at lower management levels.

White people belonged to white clubs: Pickwick, Wanderers, Carlton, YMPC and Windward, and only socialized with black people when opposing teams met. If there were black and white clubs, I cannot recall. Many English expatriates who came to the island to teach or work were warned not to join black clubs or associate socially with black people. Whites started a sport and as soon as blacks started to play that sport, they withdrew.

Anyone who broke the unspoken code and spoke about the way white people behaved was punished. He or she was ostracized not only by whites, but by blacks and more often than not the political system. I remember it took three weeks of arguing with Jimmy Cozier to get my first letter on this issue published in the *Daily News*. I also remember the fight with Robert Best to get the *Advocate* to use the word black in reference to black people.

I recall that I could not even speak to fifth form students at St. Michael's Girl School (as it was then) unless, as the headmistress said, a white man came to "rebut what I was saying." People who wore afros or natural hair were threatened with dismissal or dismissed from their jobs. There was an unholy fear in the land that retribution was at hand. Pressure was brought to bear on Errol Barrow, hence the *Public Order Act*.

I used to spend many a day at Tyrol Cot with Grantley Adams in the late sixties and I remember him telling me how the planters lobbied the Colonial Office to stop the celebration of Emancipation Day in Barbados. His son Tom confirmed how hurt his father was by this move and thought it was a reflection of white Bajans' fears. Yet, he never reinstated Emancipation Day. His administration refused to name the statue at Haggatt Hall after Bussa and preferred the vague non-specific 'Emancipation Statue'. But he (Tom) also succumbed to pressure of the white lobby by banning the burning of Mr. Harding to end the Crop Over Festival because whites complained that the ritual was being used by me to symbolically burn white people.

The present Barbados Labour Party government, under Prime Minister Owen Arthur, has reinstated Emancipation Day. And as important as this day is to remind us of the hell our ancestors went through, social gains that blacks have made are slowly being eroded once again by drawing room decisions of whites who continue to benefit enormously from the patronage of blacks without any sense of obligation or willingness to be part of a singular society. In the meantime, a black government acquiesces for fear of offending whites.

Fair is Fair

THE MESSAGE was clear. So too was the advertisement appearing in the *Sunday Advocate* in 1970. All the people in it were clear-skinned (white). It was an ad for Harrison's Department Store, No. 1 Broad Street.

The message to black people was clear too. Buy from us, but you can't advertise for us. I was adamant and called John Stanley Goddard and asked "why?". He had no answers, but it did lead to a change in Harrison's and Goddard's policy on advertising.

As a matter of fact it led to meetings between the Barbados Chamber of Commerce which John Stanley headed, and our empowerment group better known then as a Black Power group. We sought opportunities for more advancement and training of blacks in business and especially in commercial banks. John Wickham, Frank Da Silva and Elliott Mottley were independent monitors attending those discussions.

I was saddened, therefore, when I read Sir John's article in the *Business Authority* of Monday, July 6, 1998, lamenting what he calls the "complaining" of the Black Group A in the Four Square Affair and the attitude of some politicians, reporters in the Press and moderators on call-in programs.

Let me quote Sir John: "A bank has to make a judgment. If somebody comes and applies for a loan; this is not a loan to purchase, but a loan to make a down payment—$780,000, 10 percent, the bank has to make a judgment, both with regard to the collateral security and the cash flow from the project. And it has to ask: In case that project does not succeed, is there cash flow from any other sources?"

First question, Sir John: These estates were part of the Plantations Group. Were your criteria used by Royal Bank when it granted the loans to the Plantations Group? If so, what has accounted for the fact that these plantations were taken over by a receiver who has the job as auditor of Royal Bank? What happened to the required cash flow? Or were the loans based on other criteria such as traditional practices of kinship and race?

Second question: Was the second group, the one you call Group B, also trying to borrow money from Royal Bank for a downpayment? Did this Group B also approach other banks for a loan to meet the down payment? Were they given a loan by Royal Bank? If so, when? Did this group put in a bid before Group A? Did the receiver have an agreement with Group B while negotiations were still going on with Group A?

Let us look at why it is necessary for Group A to protest as vigorously as possible. The Four Square group of estates is about 2,100 acres. Based on the proposed cost, it is not profitable planting cane. It cannot be profitable for beef rearing or dairying. It can only be profitable by developing the 500 acres of rab lands associated with the plantations or by quarrying, for example, in order to clear the debt. The expected gross on these projects should not be less than $20 million.

Both Mr. Michael Power of Group A and Mr. C.O. Williams of Group B have been involved in subdivision of plantation land, dairy farming, and quarrying. Mr. Williams also specializes in beef farming.

Third question: Is it not true that

C.O. WILLIAMS

the $6.6 million will clear the debt to Royal Bank including all associated expenses? Is it not also true that with the offer of $7.8 million, shareholders in Plantations Limited may be able to share in the remaining $1.2 million which will have to be paid to Plantations Limited?

Question four: Let us go back again. Why did Royal Bank take six weeks to decide on the loan for Mr. Michael Power and why did they wait until two days before the deadline to inform him?

Question five: Why did the receiver refuse to accept the fact that Mr. Power had received the required down payment from another bank? Was the leverage of kinship at the bank a consideration? Were job security and secret agreements behind this action to stop the Power family from acquiring economic empowerment?

Question six: Do you remember hearing a story of how a man who had no assets, no collateral went into a bank and said that all he had to offer was the fact that he had eight sons who were willing to work hard? Do you remember your grandfather and Uncle Victor telling you that story? Was that decision, to quote you again, "not based on race, but based on commercial practice on law?" Could my black grandfather receive the same considerations in the 1920s? Or could the Powers in 1990?

I have written before that many white Bajans have acquired wealth through the subdivision of plantations. Blacks are entitled to do the same. But whenever they try, somebody is always putting a big rock in the road to 'brek dem foot'. I want to make it abundantly clear that I am an admirer of Mr. C.O. Williams and I know that he would not be a party to any unfair practices. But fair is fair and there is more in the Royal Bank mortar than in the pestle.

If It Ent Racism, What Is It?

AS I was telling wunna, fair is fair. I agree with Sir John Stanley Goddard that the issue should be "about broadening the base and accelerating the pace of economic empowerment for all Barbadians." That is what I am trying to do.

When Black people were finally emancipated in 1838, they had no land—no assets other than their ability to work hard. They could not even sell their labour to the highest bidder. Legislation was enacted to prevent this. Selling produce in the city and to the ships in the careenage was also prevented by legislation. Even walking on the sidewalks with a tray on your head was an offensive and prohibited act, prosecutable in court and punishable by fines or/and imprisonment.

Blacks fled the plantation tenantries for the cramped but free-er urban tenantries of Carrington Village, Green Fields, the Orleans, Alkins Land, Phillips Land, Water Hall land, Bay Land and so on. They fled the country with the permission of the white ruling elite who feared uprisings when sugar prices dropped. Many went to Guyana, Trinidad and Panama.

From Panama where they were paid in silver, hence the Silver Men, they purchased several plantations in Barbados. This is the natural inclination of any people: to own land to house their families.

It wasn't until after the riots in 1937 and Grantley Adams and the Barbados Workers' Union that there was an attempt to re-establish the dignity of a people who were exploited at every level

GRANTLEY ADAMS

by a white minority. The Moyne Commission lamented the poor housing conditions in the country. The black government that took over concentrated on providing people with better housing, education and public health.

When the opportunity arose, people bought their own land and built their own houses without the strangling concept of mortgages. These chattel houses were converted to wall from back to front as the owners' lot improved.

These properties were to become the assets which allowed the black middle class to finance several projects, including the education of their children.

Hear what Sir John has to say about this: "What has happened over the years is that black people have tended to invest in property, not in shares of public companies. This is despite the fact that there are nineteen listed public companies on the Securities Exchange of Barbados and there is absolutely no restriction as to who can own shares."

Read that statement carefully again. Note the use of "despite the fact." Implied in it is that we should not have made these investments in property and that we should have invested our money in the nineteen public companies, most of which they control. In other words, we should have invested our money in white controlled companies because there are no restrictions as to who can own shares.

Black Bajans own the majority of policies with Barbados Mutual. They are the major contributors to Pension Funds as well as to the National Insurance Fund. All three of these entities are major investors in the nineteen public companies in Barbados.

What about the management and control of these companies? Sir John is silent.

Sir John also states that "there are supposed to be 63,000 vehicles on this island and 47,000 are cars, but the white population is only about three per cent." Does that statement make sense? Yes, only if you realize that he is showing that the population of Barbados is 97 percent non-white or black.

If this is so and we know it is so, then we are buying most of the cars and for that matter, most of the goods and services being provided in the island. It is therefore Black people who are sustaining and maintaining all of these public and private companies in Barbados.

Let us look at the public companies that Sir John wants us to invest in. Remember that public companies are quite different from private companies. There are private companies like the C.O. William's Group, the Simpson Group and the Nation Group. By and large these private companies tend to do what they want, when they want, and how they want. The same is true for public companies, except that their actions must be transparent to the public and accountable to the public and the investors.

Why is it that neither of the two long serving black men has been appointed Managing Director of Roberts, a public company? What made them ineligible? What were the criteria used? Competence? Performance? Colour?

It certainly was colour when Teddy Griffith was blocked from becoming President of Mutual.

TEDDY GRIFFITH

RALPH TAYLOR

Isn't that how most of the board voted?

Will it be colour that will determine who will become Chairman and CEO of BS&T? Is Ralph Taylor's record at Almond Resorts and his monumental contribution to the profitability of BS&T not enough? Or is it that a black man is not to manage and control any of these public companies? According to the gospel of Sir John, we should invest in public companies.

Sir John has also said: "Some of us happen to be black, some of us happen to be white, not one of us is responsible for it. It all goes back to our history and ancestry—we're all Barbadians." Then what does a black man have to do to reach the top of any of these public companies?

If it ent racism, what is it?

Siege Mentality

JULIAN MURPHY was a character. He loomed large like a Bajan Buddha as he sat on his little wooden bench outside the half-dilapidated shed that I thought was a blacksmith shop on the seaside of the northern edge of Shorey Village, St. Andrew. He was shirtless. His bare chest and belly, purple as the skin of the ripe fatpork found on the sand hills around him and just as swibbly, was devoid of hair. Not so his face, which was grizzled, or his head, which reminded me of sour grass during dry season. Julian was a Bajan poor white, a red leg and a veritable encyclopaedia of the mores of Bajans in the parish of St. Andrew.

It was the late sixties or the early seventies and my quest was still to find that elusive answer to the question "who or what is a Bajan?" That search took me to St. Andrew where I was told to go and talk to Julian. And I did.

Julian was an ebullient raconteur whose language was spiced with sexual images in such abundance that the recordings I made are useless for airplay. Yet in his stories about the people of St. Andrew, a couple of things stood out. He was not tainted with any attitude of inferiority or superiority, racism or a siege mentality. His was an unapologetic display of a shared life, one in which he was a proud member.

There were many people who came around that afternoon. Little children, especially, in all sorts of colours and shapes, who Julian described as his "children children." There was no differentiation in colour. There was no separation in his mind about who they were.

He told me an apocryphal story of Mr. Gill, the white plantation owner who bought out Sedge Pond, River, Bawdens and several other plantations in St. Andrew. He also taught me the song documenting these events, interspersing them with intimate details of Mr. Gill's breeding habits.

My mind recently focussed on Julian when it was announced that a Reconciliation Committee would be established to look into race relations in Barbados.

Julian and Mr. Gill represent in many ways the oneness of what Barbados is and can be. Like A.F. Ward of Mount Gay, who demonstrated this in his own lifestyle and achievements. His progeny are no worse for it and some may argue that they are better off. But there is still a persistent influential group of whites that somehow continue to perpetuate a siege mentality based on the retention of colour as a means of survival. This is based on the

A.F. WARD

perception that whiteness is a guarantor of "beauty and truth."

Recently there has been a wholesale attempt to portray white historical circumstances of indenturedness as equivalent or worse than that of African enslavement. I for one do not wish to categorize one form of enslavement as superior or inferior to another, as all types of enslavement are horrible and cannot be justified.

But whites in Barbados have failed time and time again to understand and/or acknowledge the psychological impact of the demonization of blackness and the destruction of memory and achievement of African peoples by European ideas, ideals, philosophy and religion. Nor have those 'whites' understood the nature of the power emanating from Eurocentric biases against black people simply because, in spite of their own incarceration, they saw themselves and still see themselves as extensions of that power of whiteness. Thus, black political power is seen as meaningless and buyable through 'social acceptance' or crass economic support.

Whites in Barbados have failed to accept that the whiteness that they use to establish and retain economic power has been associated with domination, oppression and privilege. It continues unabated with the campaign against the renaming of Farley Hill Park, the absence of a white National Hero, and the removal of Nelson.

Every progressive move to consolidate Barbados as a country is met with a rear-guard action calculated to undermine the democratic exercise of political power. And often these actions are linked or threatened to be linked to North Atlantic countries as a threat to stop investment or undermine faith in the government if they, the whites, are challenged.

Until something is done about this siege mentality there will always be a distrust of the intentions of many of the leaders in the business community who use colour as a means of perpetuating control.

Do We Look Like God?

MY FATHER, Ernest Deighton Mottley, was not a modern man. I have never known him to go to the movies except on Sunday nights after church and usually only to see biblical movies like Cecil B. DeMille's productions. As usual, the whole family attended.

One of DeMille's most famous productions was *The Ten Commandments*, a monumental epic about the story of Moses. It was typical Hollywood. Grand in scale and propagandistic in tone. It projected a European view of biblical history, particularly Egypt and the Pharaohs, who were treated as extensions of Europe in image, culture and achievement.

ERNEST D. MOTTLEY

Even though I saw it around 1957/58, I remember how perfectly it fitted in with the large European sculptural figures that were installed above the entrance to the chancel of St. Mary's Church and the bas-relief stations-of-the-cross that were imbedded in the walls between its windows.

There was no doubt that the Anglican Church was permeated with a racism that it inherited from the political support it gave to slavery. And even though there were some who supported the

ST. MARY'S CHURCH

abolition of slavery, racism had already ingrained itself deep in the psyche of the congregations and administrators of the church worldwide. Indeed this attitude is still the dominant view and continues to be even in the Caribbean where the church is now being run by blacks.

I took Jaja, my five year-old son, to see *The Prince of Egypt*, an animated film about Moses, his birth and sojourn in Egypt and the exodus of Jews across the Red Sea to return to Israel.

What a revelation! The Jewish producers for the first time acknowledged a number of truths. The first of these is that the Pharaoh Seti who adopted Moses was black and his family was black. And that Moses was also black since he, Moses, saw no difference between himself and his brother Rameses. The implication of this is that the Jews of Egypt were also black, which they were. Even Moses' wife is portrayed as being even darker than he.

I remember having a discussion in 1962 with Prof. John Henrik Clark, editor of a black journal called *Freedomways*, and the late great Paul Robeson. They were emphatic that only seventy Jews went to Egypt. When the Exodus occurred, they pointed out, there were many

JOHN HENRIK CLARKE

23

thousands of Jews and they had been in Egypt for several hundred years. Prof. Clark cited a wide range of sources to support his claims.

PAUL
ROBESON

Much has happened between the making of *The Ten Commandments* and the making of *The Prince of Egypt*. Africa and its peoples in the Diaspora have asserted themselves and challenged the so-called conventional view of history. Within the United States of America, the Civil Rights Movement demanded a restructuring of the relationship between blacks and the dominant culture. The movement towards independence of former colonial territories and the assertiveness of black scholarship has redefined and made obsolete and irrelevant racist doctrines and propaganda.

So *The Prince of Egypt* is indeed a revelation and I would like to invite the clergy and the congregations of the Anglican Church to take a serious look at themselves and the doctrine (past, present and future) that underlines their faith. Even Franklyn Graham, Billy Graham's son, said that Jesus was not white.

Recently, I have been looking at the religious music of the African diaspora (Shango, Santeria, Xango, Voodoo, Kumina, Pokomania, Spiritual Baptists, Shouters, Baptists, Winti, Hindu, Islam and of course Anglicans, Roman Catholics, Methodists, Moravians, et al.). What was particularly revealing about the Anglicans, particularly in Barbados, for example, is how little indigenous music or local original music is used in their worship.

I remember that as a young chorister at St. Mary's Church, it was a rare event to sing an anthem composed by a Bajan. There were a few written by Cameron Ramsay and Charles Hinds of the Eagle Hall Village Choir. I don't remember many others. What is significant about them is that they were all written in the European classical musical genre. I came across a few

F.B. Grant
an. 1853 — August 1869

Thomas Clarke
Sept. 1869 — May 1878

E.N. Thomas
n. 1879 — Mar. 1885

C. G. Clarke Hunte
April 1892 — May 1904

Canon W.M. Grant Murray
1904—1933

ST. MARY'S CHURCH RECTORS

pieces on the St. Michael's Cathedral Choir recordings which John Fletcher had also written, and they too fell squarely within this Eurocentric tradition.

I have never heard about the Anglican Church commissioning local composers to produce music for use in its churches. At least twenty years ago I challenged the then Bishop, Drexel Gomez, on this anomaly and he admitted that it was and promised to try and correct it. It appears as if the politics of the Anglican Church in Barbados got in the way. Nothing ever became of it. Maybe now that he is Archbishop, we may see something happen.

I remember being told by an old woman in St. George that she and her friends preferred to attend the Anglican Church Army meetings that were held on Wednesday nights, where Sankeys were sung and they got a chance to march (dance?) around the community singing and beating tambourines (drums?).

That is the music, what about the images in St. Mary's Church and beyond? How many artists have been commissioned to produce works of art for the churches? Did God make us in his own image?

How about it, Bishop Rufus, Harold Critchlow and Jimmy Springer? Did he?

Perceptions

"If I am different to how you perceive me, then you are not what you think you are."

James Baldwin

WE WERE scheduled to leave on Sunday at midnight. There were four of us. Three white. One woman. One black. Me. Our destination—Little Rock, Arkansas. The year was 1958.

We were selected by the University of Manitoba student newspaper, the Manitoban, to go to Little Rock. Governor Oval E. Faubus, in 1957, had resisted integration of the Little Rock Central High School by dispatching the Arkansas National Guard to block the nine black students from entering the school.

All over the South there was wholesale resistance to integration in education as demanded by the US Supreme Court in the landmark case *Brown versus the Board of Education.* The doctrine of separate schools for whites and separate schools for blacks was ruled "separate but not equal." We were to investigate

FAUBUS' SOLDIERS CARRYING
BLACKS TO SCHOOL

FAUBUS AND RACISM IN
LITTLE ROCK, ARKANSAS

and report on the situation.

At one minute to midnight, Louis Tull asked me what to tell my father when I didn't return. I decided to stay in Winnipeg.

Winnipeg is the heart of Canada. It was a white Anglo-Saxon-Protestant town, lush with the ignorance of isolation and self-righteous prejudices against Jews, Catholics, American Indians, European immigrants and their countries, and blacks of all descriptions and origin.

LOUIS TULL

Every other person was an immigrant from Europe. Not many blacks lived there. There were four sets of blacks: a few indigenous Canadian blacks hidden on the other side of the railway tracks; a handful of black American football players; a basket of Caribbean women working as domestics; and

27

several conspicuous black students (this sometimes included a few creolized Trinidadian and Guyanese Indians) from the Caribbean and Africa.

We learned for the first time that we had tails, lived in trees, never used knives and forks, never wore shoes or clothes, and travelled from our grass-hut homes by donkey cart. This contrasted sharply with our own knowledge of Canada, its major cities, exports and imports and of how many Caribbean people fought for Canada in the Royal Canadian Air Force.

Students at the university tolerated our presence, but there were many students (including men) who went beyond toleration to become good friends with Caribbean students.

Getting and holding housing off campus, however, was a very difficult situation as many of the immigrants who seemed to control the housing in Winnipeg always gave us the "we never rent to those" argument when they discovered we were black. In retrospect, I believe we changed Winnipeg in many ways, particularly as more and more Caribbean students came.

Four years later I decided to move to New York and to do so by bus. I wanted to go as far South as I dared, since I never got to make that journey in 1958.

I boarded a Greyhound bus in Winnipeg. It was a split level bus and I took the right front seat of the upper level where I had an unrestricted view of the road ahead. There were only a few of us on that bus. It didn't take us long to be on the highway heading South. As the sky became translucent and the land around the highway became visible, I was surprised to see how flat the countryside was. Endless farmland with an occasional cluster of trees or buildings in the distance. Our last stop in Canada was Emerson, Manitoba.

The US side of the border was not very different. We passed some tiny hamlets and picked up passengers on the road. We stopped in Grand Forks and Fargo, North Dakota. Then it was the twin cities of Minneapolis and St. Paul in Minnesota.

The road to Chicago was linked by a number of small towns. The bus seemed not to stop at each. It was amazing to see how many people got on the bus and then got off rather than sit next to me. Finally, at one stop, a white soldier boarded and, after hesitating for a moment, he sat down next to me.

Although it was a full seat, he scotched on the edge of the seat with the right side of his botsie, while the left was hanging in mid air in the aisle. When I realized what was happening, I made myself more comfortable by spreading out myself and took up what extra space there was.

There was no conversation between us. At times he sat sideways with his back to me. He kept getting up and going to the driver. As morning broke, the driver announced that we would be making a rest stop soon and we would be able to use the bathrooms and purchase breakfast.

Needless to say, I got neither service nor access to a toilet. I did as a Bajan would do: cussed and found a tree.

I fumed on the way back to the bus, asking if we were in Alabama or Mississippi. There was total silence on the bus and the same amount of stares. The soldier who sat next to me returned and to my surprise came and sat down fully on the seat and offered me coffee and donuts.

I was startled, but it started a conversation between us. Then he said to me "I didn't realize that you were not a nigger." And before I could answer, he said, "I only realized that you were British when you were talking in the diner."

He had never had a discussion with a black man before. He had never heard about the Caribbean or Africa. Nor did he understand the relationship between Africa and Europe or between Africa and America. The only reason he thought I was British was the fact that my accent was not Southern. The only blacks he heard about were slaves in the South. We talked through the night.

We arrived in Chicago early the next morning. Unlike Winnipeg and all dem other towns, it was a black town. As we disembarked, he shook my hand and thanked me profusely for opening his eyes.

I wonder if Baldwin was right!

Bim

"Black economic marginalisation, unless addressed urgently with the full support of all stakeholders, will serve to subvert all our best efforts at nation building. We simply do not have the time to allow the notion of black second class economic citizenship to fester within the context of a rapidly growing economy that is seen as a dream world for white entrepreneurs."

Prof. Hilary Beckles - "Mr. Arthur's Project: Why Barbados must Lead," at the Annual Conference of the Barbados Labour Party October 30, 1999

THERE WAS a joke gine round fuh years bout how Barbados send and tell England to guh long and fight Germany cause Bimshire people was behind them. I hope wunna understand that it was the white people who saw demself and Barbados as a county of England! Hence Bimshire. Although I must say that there was some poor-great black people who did feel so too.

Not James A. Tudor though. James A. did tell me that when he was gine downtown to volunteer in the 1914-18 world war and join Barney Miller and the rest of the gang, he overhear a white man saying "Let them niggers guh long and kill duhself. I ent gine nuh way." James A. turn back. He ent went nowhere neither.

JAMES A. TUDOR

But remember that Bim is an African word meaning 'we people, we family'. Wunna should read Dr. Richard Allsopp's

DR. RICHARD ALLSOP

Dictionary of Caribbean English Usage. White people learn bout Bim when dem learn how to talk while sucking black woman bubby. The wet nurse. And they take it, as they should, and make it part of their own, not our own, dem own. When Dipper was thinking that "We now have a country," we became dem country.

And that night, thirty-three years ago, in the flood-lit darkness of the Garrison Savannah, where grass was dying from suffocating feet, with showers of blessing washing tears of hope from thousands of cheekbones, the Union Jack came down and the Trident fly up high canonized by voices coarsened by the joys of tomorrow.

And I was the first out of the blocks like I was stepping barefoot pon a hot soft tar-road when Captain Peter Short get on as if nothing did change. First he said to Don Norville, "Barbados was an ideal country and the Pollock Brothers should be allowed to play for the Rest of the World vs Barbados and so dem could see how good white people and black people does live here." The second point he make was bout the segregated cricket clubs of Pickwick, Wanderers, Carlton, YMPC, Leeward and Winward. "Don't push us [to change], give us our good time!" And for daring to tell him the truth, I was called a racist. It in de papers. Wuk was hard to come by after that.

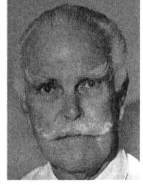

PETER SHORT

But it is strange how after thirty-three years of Independence we seemingly still in the same place with a National Reconciliation Commission.

A couple of years later, 1968 or 1969, I find out that Continental telephone was jukking we in we eye to the tune of 800 percent increases with the connivance of Barbados Shipping and Trading (BS&T), Goddards and Plantations Limited. the *Advocate*, under pressure refused to print the names of the Directors of BS&T and Plantations, and the shareholders of the Telephone Company who was sitting on the Public Utilities Board and was auditors of the company. Insider works. I hit the streets with public meetings.

Today um is still de same. More insider trading and special deals, whether pon money or pon rum. Nepotism in public company contracts wid lorries or bottle caps. Amazing to see holes get dig out and full back up by third gangs. Threatening phone calls to newspapers and cutting of advertising. And wuk hard to come by even fuh frighten lawyers.

Where are the protestors, the voices of meaningful dissent? Disappearing in the forests of inclusion? Silence. The left turning anti-clockwise like a dog trying to catch he tail. And the Pan-Africanist fuhget that Pan-Africanism born here in Bim. Even Eric Sealy like Humpty Dumpty fall into a quarry off a wall. And everybody frighten to offend the white man when he practise anti-Bim attitudes. But duppy know who to frighten!

And white people getting everyting dem want. If white people want to buy cane-ground, dem can buy cane-ground. If white people want to sell dem cane-ground, dem can sell dem cane ground. If black people want to sell dem cane-ground, dem must suck salt and wait. If black people want to buy cane-ground, hell brek loose. Remember when a black try to build five golf courses pon plantation land? Or buy Foursquare?

Black people from Africa settled involuntarily in Barbados and other parts of the Caribbean and the New World and brought with them a sense of compassion, a compassion laced with a traditional religiosity that has remained embedded in generation after generation of black pride. We din tek rain thirty-three years ago fuh nothing.

Ah wonder if in the twenty-first century Bim will ever mean the same thing to everybody?

The Rightness of Whiteness, Part 1

THE RECENT bassa-bassa at Barbados Shipping and Trading Company brings sharply into focus the continuing disproportionate dominance of the business sector by white Bajan businessmen. Not in terms of numbers, but in the allocation of financial resources and the access to the corridors of power to obtain favourable decisions.

There are two other aspects to this dominance that need critical examination: employment practices and the glass ceiling, and the myth of white success.

In making these comments, I want all and sundry to understand clearly that I do not grudge or envy their successes, past, present or future. The reality of what has been happening for the last century and a half must not be carried into the twenty-first century. The existing situation must undergo some major adjustment.

Thirty years ago when I spoke out on these matters, I was deemed a racist, a hazard for the course. However, it did result in some changes, some cosmetic and some substantial. I hope that these comments will provoke some positive action towards the obvious and lasting solution.

Let us start with the allocation of financial resources.

When Sir John Stanley Goddard was recapping the founding of Goddard enterprises by his grandfather, J.N Goddard, and his uncle, Victor Goddard in 1921, he pointed out that they were able to walk into CIBC and obtain a loan on the security of nine sons and one daughter who were willing to work hard to repay the loan. They did.

Very admirable, but was Horace King's father with his thirteen children able to do the same? If he could have, maybe instead of leaving a meagre blacksmith shop, he may have been able to leave a substantial steel construction business like the Warrens Group.

I don't know of a single black man who can recount such a story. I do know that white solicitors of the past used to act as bankers to the wealthy and grant unsecured mortgages and loans to blacks usually for the purchase of land or houses. However, those who benefitted from such were few and far between and generally were clients of the solicitor.

The white management of the banks made life easier for most whites than it did for blacks. This was especially so since most of the whites in business were importing goods from the bank's parent country. Even when James A. Tudor had his network of over ninety shops island-wide, he still had to depend on primary importers for goods and credit. No credit was available from the banks and it was difficult to become an agent for English firms.

However, a white person could get off a boat, walk straight into a bank and obtain a loan to buy a car, to set up a business or even buy a house. This is not far-fetched. There are several examples of this. Unfortunately, even when some of the bank managers were black, the same situation occurred. I don't know if they were reacting to 'His Master's Voice', but they certainly acted more stringently than even the master. It wasn't until the banks changed their employment practices and indigenous banks became a reality that we have seen an easing of the situation.

In the late fifties when Bank of Nova Scotia first came to Barbados, it granted consumer loans to black Bajans with little discrimination. It didn't take long before they changed that policy. It was contrary to the policies of the other Banks— Barclays, Royal and CIBC. No doubt the decision to stop this 'enrichment' of blacks was made in some drawing room.

By and large then, whites were able to tap into the savings of black Bajans far more easily than blacks could tap into their own savings. This is not to suggest that whites didn't have savings, but most of their savings were invested in real estate, businesses and other assets.

From these loans whites were able to fund additional projects, successfully or unsuccessfully. These loans allowed them to establish a track record with the banks which made it easier to tap into further loans.

In the sixties and seventies, a number of black businessmen were able to get loans from the Barbados Development Bank, a government statutory corporation, to start a few manufacturing businesses. Most of this funding went to plant and equipment. To get working capital, they had to turn to the commercial banks.

In order to get loans, blacks were required to pledge insurance policies and car and house and land and anything that had value. Notice I said 'and' and not 'or'. Recall the demonstrations at the banks. There are many black businessmen who can testify to value of the loan. The assumption was that they owned or had access to all of these things. The ground rules for blacks were different and if they got the loan, it was given in dribbles.

When the time came where a more substantial loan was required to expand the operation in order to get economies of scale, bruggadung, all fall down. The bank policy was to literally limit the size and operation of the black-owned business. This was the horror story of the seventies and the disadvantages they faced.

How did whites acquire so much capital? There are several

reasons. The first is inheritance. They were either inheritors within the merchant class or the planter class. In both cases, real estate is or was a major common factor: prime properties in Bridgetown, plantations across the country.

Several owners of plantations have been able to leverage them into cash by selling off rab lands or subdividing the total plantation into smaller agricultural lots or residential lots. The profits from these sales have been plowed into alternative investments in and out of Barbados, into hotels, and into new and/or additional businesses. Many of these subdivisions were consented to by government. This means that they had access to the corridors of power.

It is my belief that their 'whiteness' played a major role in gaining the access and in obtaining the decisions for the subdivisions. That is as far as I want to go with respect to that. At another time I will go into further details on plantations, their owners and the developers.

In contrast, few blacks have been able to benefit in the same way. They were limited to subdivisions in large agricultural lots with whites getting the more lucrative residential subdivision permission.

One final point. There are whites who worked hard and efficiently with what they got. Others have not. Given a level playing field, I have no doubt that we would have seen even greater successes by black businessmen had they had access to financial resources like whites.

The Rightness of Whiteness, Part 2

LAST WEEK I wrote about the continuing disproportionate dominance of the business sector by white Bajan businessmen, not in terms of numbers, but in the allocation of financial resources and the access to the corridors of power to obtain favourable decisions.

It is interesting to look at the historical use in this century of the plantation and how it was used to create and extend the wealth of its owners. In spite of the vicissitudes and fortunes of sugar, the merchant arm of the conglomerate sucked the plantations dry like a soucouyan.

Both Plantations Limited and Barbados Shipping and Trading made sure that companies controlled by their directors purchased materials and supplies from the parent/associated company whether they were needed or not. For example, in more recent years tyres were required for tractors, trucks, trailers, pickups, and cars yearly as part of the soucouyan process.

In addition, the management structure ensured that kith and kin were employed. The many tiered levels were capped by an attorney who acted as overall manager in lieu of the owners. A contrast to this type of operation is Friendship Plantation, owned and operated by Patrick Bethel. He is farmer, he is management, he is worker. The same

PATRICK BETHEL

applies to my under-sexed friend Richard
Hoad. The record shows that where such
farms are structured in this way, the
operation is more profitable.

RICHARD HOAD

The plantation continued to be a source
of financial well-being. Vegetables and
ground provisions used in intercropping
were seldom included in the revenues
accruing to the plantation. Even insurance
money from fields destroyed by cane-fires
never made it to the coffers. Remember
when the Minister of Agriculture, Johnny
Cheltenham, openly accused planters of a
policy of arson for profit!

Then there were the migrants from the
plantations who sold off the Plantation
Houses and invested the revenues in
hotels, transferring bad management
practices from agriculture to tourism.
And lest we forget, the monies borrowed
from the Agricultural Bank and then

JOHNNY
CHELTENHAM

subsequently the Barbados National Bank, for fertilizers to grow
cane and sugar, instead grew hotel beds and rum punches.

When all the profits were used up and the hotel plant was run
down and there was no more Plantation House to sell or fertilizer
to be had, they ran to government for help and got it. Plantations
Limited stumbled and faltered, and only Lawrence Duprey and
CLICO salvaged some of the owners' pride.

Barbados Shipping and Trading tried a big-foot move and
amalgamated all the plantations with encumbrances, removed
them from within the conglomerate and attempted to unload
them on the government through the Barbados National Bank.

They nearly succeeded in passing this empty shell over to the government in a very sophisticated shell game. It was worthy of the Garrison on Gold Cup Day. Fortunately, BS&T had to accept responsibility for the debts.

Finally, subdivision of the plantation land was to provide the real source of wealth for old and new owners. I will treat with that in greater detail in a separate article sometime in the future.

Another means of accumulating wealth is monopoly. And Goddards has been a past-master at this. If Goddards is not involved in a monopoly, then check, it is an oligopoly with only two or three other players in the game and only a matter of time before Goddards is the only game in town.

Let me run down some of the enterprises, past and present:

- Flight Kitchen at the Adams Airport
- BICO - Cold Storage and Ice Cream
- Detergent Manufacturing
- Pork Processing
- Duty-Free Shopping (with Cave Shepherd, Colombian Emeralds, Bridgetown Port)
- Ship Chandlery (Supplying ships e.g., Tourist Liners)
- Rum Manufacturing
- Beer Manufacturing
- Bread Making
- Pine Hill Dairy
- Insecticides (McBride)

It would appear that one of the reasons why Goddards got out of their core business of food retailing was the stiffness of the competition, especially from the mushrooming small black entrepreneurs. Some of these black entrepreneurs have fallen by the wayside, but some are still there and growing: Julie'N,

Jordans, Shamrock, Budgbuy, Eddies, Carlton, et al. Is Goddards capable of surviving in an open competitive environment?

If some of these black entrepreneurs were to enjoy some of the privileges that whites enjoy from the banking sector and from government, they would also be outstanding. Those who have been able to get this support are demonstrating clearly superior management since they are neither involved in monopolies or oligopolies.

Monopolies and oligopolies make sense to those who operate them. In the context of Barbados, it allows those with advantage to continually outpace their competitors. Is government contributing to the building of such monopolies and/or oligopolies? Not in all cases, but in some. Take the Bridgetown Port, for example. Government had an opportunity of creating something different, but instead allowed themselves to be persuaded into creating the present situation at the Port.

It is this sharing on this tight little island of ours that is missing. There is a greed, guided by an advantage of colour, a legacy of slavery and European dominance. Rational men and women must recognize that we share a common heritage. We must grow together, not apart.

The Rightness of Whiteness Part 3, or Where the Soul Goes, the Cash Flows

REGINALD GRANT Barrow graduated from Codrington College as a minister of the Anglican Church in the first decade of the 20th century. Barrow looked forward to becoming a deacon and expected to be assigned to a church in Barbados. Unfortunately, he was not. He was encouraged to go down the Islands or to West Africa as a missionary. He refused to do either.

The Anglican Church was an extension of the plantation and there was no room for a young, radical black priest. Codrington College was part of the plantation and students were not expected to come out radical. As a matter of fact, even though it was no longer fashionable to stamp CC (Christopher Codrington) in the chest of blacks, it was expected to be circumscribed in their brains instead.

That is why work in the islands or Africa was recommended. A black priest was to be a civilizing tool, a vehicle of Christianity as defined by Europe. When the Rev. Reginald Grant Barrow stared into the looking glass at himself, he saw in that mirror image the end of his pursuit.

Rev. Barrow decided to become a teacher and applied for the vacant position of headmaster of the Alleyne School. The Alleyne School was set up by a trust left by Sir John Gay Alleyne to educate poor white boys in St. Andrew. When Rev. Barrow took over Alleyne School there were six students left. As Rev Barrow explained to me, "I know that they were planning to shut down the school and blame me."

The headmaster of the Alleyne School was also Secretary to the St. Andrew Vestry. Rev. Barrow promptly set out to read everything they had on the school and the functioning of the vestry. He quickly discovered that the planters had taken most of the money from the Alleyne Trust and used it to pave the roads to their plantations and for other 'unauthorized' things.

Rev. Barrow set on a scheme to keep the Alleyne School open by extending the enrolment. He invited all the primary schools in St. Andrew to send their best black students to the school, thus increasing the numbers and pre-empting any possibility of closure. By threatening to reveal the infelicities with the Alleyne Trust to the public, his actions were reluctantly supported and the Alleyne School survived.

I tell this story because although Codrington College produced many priests over the years, there was a glass ceiling in place preventing a Black Bajan from becoming first a rector at a Parish Church and subsequently Bishop. After Independence, the Anglican Church finally chose a black Bahamian, Drexel Gomez, to become Bishop.

The Anglican Church was not unlike the business sector in Barbados. Many blacks have been employed in several firms, large private and public companies, and regardless of their ability, they were never ever able to become the boss, particularly if the company was white-owned.

The highest ranking job in many of these companies is the Human Resource Director (HRD). To be a little facetious, this is the modern day equivalent to the driver on the plantation during slavery. It is a patronizing and contemptuous decision to box blacks into the most non-threatening positions.

Please don't think I am deprecating the role of an HRD specialist. I am not. I am lamenting the decision of how and why the 'Personnel Director' is appointed. In many cases, the recommendations of this HRD person is never followed, since in many cases senior management appointments are based not on ability, but on nepotism.

It is easier for a Trevor Clarke (BARTEL) and a Vince Yearwood (BET) to rise to the top in a International company like Cable and Wireless than in a local company. Recall the intensive lobby to prevent Teddy Griffith from being appointed president of Mutual.

Look at the banks in Barbados and you can see the glass ceiling clearly and distinctly. Sometimes I wonder why it is that Barclay's Bank, CIBC, Nova Scotia and Royal Bank have never seen the wisdom of appointing black CEOs like in Jamaica and Trinidad. I know of Bajans and Antiguans and Jamaicans who are the contemporaries of black bankers in Barbados who are CEOs of Banks in Jamaica which are bigger than all the banks in Barbados put together. Is it pressure from their big clients in Barbados that prevents this?

Let me return to the Church for a moment. And maybe this is symptomatic of the fear or mistrust or siege mentality that exists. When Rev. Hatch was Rector of St. James Parish Church, did you ever notice the number of baptisms, weddings and communions he used to perform for white Bajans? It seems that there was a sudden migration away from the other Anglican Churches. Others found comfort with Holmes Williams or William Cuke or Archbishop Dickson.

The point is that there is a reluctance to let blacks manage the cash or the soul.

The Rev. Reginald Grant Barrow went on to become a Bishop in the church wing of the Marcus Garvey Movement. I wonder if these experiences influenced his son Errol Walton Barrow to disestablish the Anglican Church. Errol Barrow refused to give Bajan women the same rights as Bajan men to prevent what he called "the importation of new management." Rev Barrow's stepson, Henry deBoulay Forde, changed his stepbrother's policy and gave Bajan women the same rights as men.

Where the soul goes, the cash flows!

Don Bizzy, Family & Stakeholders

"Businessmen Sir Charles Williams and his brother Ralph 'Bizzy' Williams presented him (Obadele) with the documentation that will ensure him gifts of land and shares, respectively. Oba has received a prime plot of elevated land in Millennium Heights, St. Thomas, from C.O. Williams Construction and 5,000 shares in Williams' Industries. Shortly after he presented Oba with a share certificate and an annual report on Williams' Industries, Bizzy Williams jovially remarked he hoped that Oba would learn a lot about the company as he was now a stakeholder."

Mike King reporting in the Saturday Sun
Saturday October 7, 2000

IN THE process of the colonization of Barbados by the English, forced labour consisting of extremely poor British subjects were used. Many of these persons indentured themselves for five to seven years while some were abducted and 'Barbadosed' without their consent.

The white planters developed a system of white servitude with respect to these indentured servants completely controlling their lives, mistreating them severely and brutally. Poor white indentureship was used as a practice wicket for African slavery. Some of these poor whites left Barbados for freedom in South Carolina and other states in the USA. Those who remained were 'trapped' by the nature of their circumstance and abject poverty.

When African slavery became the dominant system of employment in the shift to sugar cultivation, Africans given or took over all the major tasks on the plantation: weeding. planting, reaping, blacksmithing, tool making, carpentry, stone working, furniture and cabinet making. What this meant was that poor whites became more and more marginalized.

As a matter of fact, things got so bad that after many decades the same planters had to create a special technical school for training poor whites in some of the same skills. And many of the so-called older secondary schools were started in order to give them an education.

Many of the large plantations were taken over by merchants in the first part of the 20th Century. We see first the evolution of the Cotton Factory Group (now defunct), then Plantations Limited and then Barbados Shipping and Trading. These last two groupings were the major recipients of plantation land. Most of this land is now in the hands of newer companies: Colonial Life Insurance Company (CLICO) from Trinidad and Barbados Farms, a 'bad' company isolated from BS&T, respectively. Of course, Sir Charles is a major owner of plantation land too.

Dr. Cecilia Karch Brathwaite, in her partially delivered Emancipation 2000 lecture, "Transformation? Or Modification of White Society in Barbados" pointed out that during this same period when the white merchants were taking over the plantations, poor whites were moving from the country areas to Bridgetown and its immediate environs. More importantly, they were also being given priority of employment at all of the businesses in Bridgetown and Speightstown (white, then brown-skinned with straight hair, and brown-skinned without.)

Let me quote Karch:

> While merchants were paying pittance to their workers, nevertheless, there continued to be a stream of white migrants coming in from St. John, St. Phillip, St. Andrew and St. Lucy desperate for employment; and white collar positions conferred a relatively high status in an economy predicated on agricultural labour. This form of mobility for white working class men and women is a

pertinent example of manipulation of the labour market that becomes a controlling mechanism. Holding out the carrot of upward mobility for working class whites in the increasing important commercial sector solidified domination by the white community, as it separated the white working class from the black, forming in effect 'an aristocracy of labour'. Equally important, the ideology of racial inequality and the necessity of its perpetuation were strengthened.

In other words, in spite of the bad treatment meted out to poor whites, they still saw themselves as white and a part of the whole superstructure, albeit at the bottom. There was and still is an expectation that the whites who head up these companies or any other company have an obligation to employ them and protect them. And in essence this is what happens. But it goes further. An examination of business practices over the last 40 years would also show that many floundering or bankrupt small white-owned businesses were taken over by large public corporations more by way of benevolence than on solid business practices.

I have noted that both BS&T and Williams' Industries have created in-house Public Relations and Advertising Divisions to promote their images and their products. I think it would be superfluous for me to identify the managers of these units. About two months ago, Mr. Bizzy Williams of Williams' Industries (and I would like to congratulate Bizzy on his award as Caribbean Entrepreneur of the Year), pointed out that both C.O. Williams Construction and Williams' Industries were family businesses and hence all or nearly all of the senior managers were part of the family, a seemingly extended family.

There are some questions arising from the report quoted above that I would like to put to Don Bizzy. Are the shareholders of Williams' Industries the only stakeholders? Are the employees, customers and clients of Williams' Industries also stakeholders too and can they get to study the Annual Reports also? Would Oba qualify for a management job at Williams' Industries? And is Williams' Industries going public or is this all a public relations kadoo?

Let My People Go!

"The problem of the Twentieth Century is the problem of the colour-line - the relation of the darker to the lighter races of men in Asia and Africa, in America and the islands of the sea."

W.E.B. DuBois

PROFESSOR W.E.B. DuBois, a black American, was the most formidable black thinker and scholar at the beginning of the twentieth century. He was a graduate of Fisk University in 1888 before spending four years at Harvard studying psychology, philosophy and history. From 1892-94, he studied economic history at the University of Berlin. He returned to Harvard to finish his doctorate and his thesis *The Suppression of the African Slave Trade* which was published as the first volume of the then new Harvard Historical Studies in 1896.

And as we enter the twenty-first century, these words remain as true today as they were one hundred years ago.

DuBois had great difficulty following the changing definitions of race and defined himself "not by physical or 'racial' heredity, but by cultural processes, that African consciousness… passed on from one generation to another." (Richard B. Moore)

In his autobiography, *Dusk of Dawn*, Dr. DuBois wrote:

> Since then the concept of race has so changed and presented so much of contradiction that as I face Africa I ask myself: what is it between us that constitutes a tie which I can feel better than I can explain? Africa is of course my fatherland. Yet neither my father nor my

father's father ever saw Africa or cared overmuch for it. My mother's folk were closer and yet their direct connection, in culture and race, became tenuous; still, my tie to Africa is strong. On this vast continent was born and lived a large portion of my direct ancestors going back a thousand years or more.

But one thing is sure and that is the fact that since the fifteenth century these ancestors of mine and their other descendants have had a common history; having suffered a common disaster and have one long memory. The actual ties of heritage between the individuals of this group vary with the ancestors that they have in common and many others: Europeans and Semites, perhaps Mongolians, certainly Indians. But the physical bond is least and the badge of colour relatively unimportant save as a badge; the real essence of this kinship is its social heritage of slavery; the discrimination and insult; and this heritage binds together not simply the children of Africa, but extends through yellow Asia and into the South Seas. It is this unity that draws me to Africa.

And the same is true about us Bajans. We, black and white, share many things in common. A heritage of enslavement. Some are too ashamed of this past to acknowledge it. Like cane fields we were cultivated and manured with inferiority. Both black and white. As blacks we have not been able to shake off the definitions because they were and still are the fundamental base of a worldwide facade of racism. For whites it was easy to pass into the ruling echelons on the basis of whiteness and money.

And yet we share a common heritage, family trees as solid as baobabs, as tall as royal palms and as broad as bearded fig trees. The faith in ourselves as Bim people is not there. We are relying on the symbols of slavery, on the tenets of racism, however subtle, to chart our destiny. There are bonds that bind us together for better or for worse. We share Gary Sobers and George Challenor, Rohan Kanhai and George Headley. Gladstone Holder, in a recent article in *Action*, recounted how whites in the George Challenor stand booed George Headley (whose father was a Bajan) in 1948 when he appealed for light against the MCC. His father cried in shame. Was this the action of King Dyall eccentrics or something deeper?

And when E. Keith Walcott refused an offer of blood from his black doctor, Dr. Coppers Clarke, for one of his grandchildren on the grounds that he did not want any black blood in his grandchild's veins, was it scientific or historical ignorance or neither?

Dean Harold Critchlow relates the story of the white priests who were always asked by families to attend funeral services of Bajan whites at the St. Michael's Cathedral and the shock of discovering that they did not know the deceased. Were the priests present to make sure that the dead were not sent to hell or to guarantee that they were put on the right path to heaven or something else?

And then there was Ralph Taylor, and Nelson, and National Heroes, and Farley Hill.

And so to a National Reconciliation Commission.

O God, let my people go! Is it going to be in this the twenty-first century?

Time To Pay Up
For the Humiliation

MY OLE man (Ernest Deighton Mottley), like a lot of young men in the 1920s, went to work as a seaman. His brother Bunny was also a seaman and drowned at sea after saving the Captain's son who fell overboard during a squall.   After several trips and spurred on by a fight in the galley, he left his last ship in Charleston, South Carolina, a port that has an association with Barbados going all the way back to the seventeenth century. South Carolina's first seven governors were white Bajans.

Nicknamed 'Rugged' in his youth, he exuded what his good friend Graham Small used to call 'ponksiness'—attitude. So Rugged decided to head to New York by bus to see his mother and the same said Graham Small and other friends. He bought his ticket at the bus depot, entered the bus and promptly sat in the front seat across from the driver. This was South of the Mason-Dixon line, an imaginary demarcation that separated the South from the North. On that day in the 1920s, he was on the wrong side of the Mason-Dixon line.

Needless to say, he was ordered by the driver to vacate the seat as the front seats of the bus were reserved for whites only. He was told to take his black ass to the back of the bus. Rugged was not going to be humiliated. He refused and argued that his money was the same as the 'white people wun' and that he was entitled to sit where he liked.

The bus driver drove the bus straight to a police station where the same order was given to him. And as was expected, Rugged proceeded to argue his case. In the middle of the argument, the cop, his hands on his gun, asked him if he was a Geechee.

A Geechee is an inhabitant of the Georgia Sea Islands off the coast of Georgia and South Carolina in the United States of America. Geechees speak 'gullah', a language indigenous to the Sea Islands off the coast of South Carolina and Georgia. They sound like Caribbean people and that is why the policeman asked Rugged if he was a Geechee. When the policeman discovered that he was from Barbados, his attitude changed simply because in his mind Rugged wasn't a nigger.

Mary A. Twining has studied Gullah and the Geechee people. With her husband Keith E. Baird and the late Prof. John Henrik Clarke, she wrote *Sea Island Roots: African Presence in the Carolinas and Georgia.* Here was a people who, like the Saramaka and the Djuka of Suriname, built an alternative existence independent of the plantation. The tragedy of slavery is that it robbed our ancestors of their right to a normal existence like other peoples and left us with a legacy of humiliation.

Professor Keith E. Baird is a Barbadian and a linguist who speaks at least ten languages. In a recent interview with the *Nation*'s North American editor, Tony Best, Professor Baird argued that African peoples in the new world should receive reparations from the European nations who engaged in and benefitted from the slave trade and plantations slavery. He further argues that those whites across the Caribbean who were also abducted and enslaved as 'bond-servants' should also be compensated similarly. I agree with him.

The African Reparations Movement has six aims and objectives:

To use all lawful means to obtain Reparations for the enslavement and colonization of African people in Africa and in the African Diaspora.

To use all lawful means to secure the return of African artifacts from whichever place they are currently held.

To seek an apology from western governments for the enslavement and colonization of African people.

To campaign for an acknowledgment of the contribution of African people to World history and civilization.

To campaign for an accurate portrayal of African history and thus restore dignity and self-respect to African people.

To educate and inform African youth, on the continent and in the Diaspora, about the great African cultures, languages and civilizations.

What are the precedents for this compensation? Jews receive millions every year from the German government and corporations as reparations for the suffering of Jewish people under the Nazi oppression during the Holocaust.

The Koreans received reparations from the Japanese for the cruelties perpetrated upon them during the Second World War. British prisoners of war received compensation from the Japanese for their treatment in prisoner of war camps. British Prime Minister John Major returned to the Japanese to ask for more compensation, as they felt that they had not received enough.

The Maoris of New Zealand recently received an apology

from the Queen of England and part payment of a claim for reparations for damage done to the Maori people during British colonial rule.

American Indians received compensations from the US, as did Japanese Americans who were imprisoned during the Second World War by the Roosevelt government.

One hundred and sixty years after emancipation and we are still suffering humiliation because of our color and our use of language. It is time for change.

Down Taw, Nuh Brush

Down Taw, Nuh Brush!

THEY WERE dressed in white. White dresses. White hats. White shoes. White gloves. They marched in single file looking neither left, nor right. High-stepping like leghorn fowls, their Evening-in-Paris perfume cascading the nostrils of sidewalk lymers juicing their imaginations with impossible dreams.

Heading the line, without a backward glance, was an overweight bantam cock by the name of Harrywills. A former boxer. A butcher. A political canvasser. A nightclub proprietor. The owner and operator of Harry's Nitery.

Of course Harrywills was not his right name, but that was the name he took when he was a boxer. It was the name of an American boxer that he admired. Everybody called him Harrywills. Not Harry, not Wills, and certainly not Mr. Wills. Just Harrywills.

Harrywills had this ritual of marching his employees up and down Broad Street on Saturday mornings to advertise Harry's Nitery. They were eight girls, sometimes ten. Among them the fantastic Dinah the Body, the headless wonder. The girl who worked wonders. The girl whose movements were known to raise the dead.

Harrywills was an illusionist. He projected the purity of his charges. He flaunted them to all and sundry. He titillated the imagination. They were like mannequins in Fogarty's show windows. To be seen, not touched!

And indeed, it was almost impossible to get into Harry's Nitery

BAY STREET

to see them or touch them. You only heard the rumours.

Like Peter at the gates of heaven, Harrywills monitored every guest from the window above the downstairs door of Harry's Nitery on Bay Street. You couldn't get in if Harrywills 'look down pon yuh and say no'. You had to be respectable, to be somebody. Young men especially did not qualify. Ordinary sailors, Yankee sailors, drunking tourists (white or black), some politicians, and particularly calypsonians were definitely not respectable enough to get in.

Sparrow was one. He immortalized the Nitery in a song called *Harry's Piggery.*

The two thugs at the door, one with a bull pizzle and the other with a guava tree stick, enforced the law. The law of Harrywills. And many a man get lash for trying to stow-way—in the back with the bull pizzle or on the waterline with the guava stick without reference to Queensbury or Johnson rules.

Once admitted, you were greeted at the top of the stairs by a wall of pictures that featured Harrywills with the likes of Ambassador Averill Harriman, former governor of New York; Lord Avon, former Prime Minister of England; the Governor of Barbados; Joan Crawford, movie star; Louis Armstrong, Jazz Musician; Prime Ministers and Mayors from all over the world; Admirals and Captains from the United States Navy, the British Navy and the Canadian Navy; and a host of other well-known international personalities.

Harry's Nitery was famous all over the world and was mentioned in many US and English papers. Its notoriety as a club that featured topless and bottomless dancers was noted as a must for all who came to Barbados. Many came to be stimulated by an evening of games. But only the girls could play.

What a sight! One after the other the girls came out, their nude bodies oily and shiny, glistening with the blues and reds of the lights around the perimeter of the room. Their supple bodies ranging from the nubile to the voluptuous. Round and round they danced, brown girls in a ring.

Then there was 'Hiddy Biddy, shut up yuh lap tight tight'. And deep into each patron's lap went hand after hand leaving an imaginary rockstone. It didn't matter whose lap. Man or woman. Once you were there, you were part of the game.

And all the time Harrywills, with mike in hand, admonished the audience about what they could do and couldn't do. "You could touch, you could feel but don't damage the merchandise with unclean fingernails."

This was followed by an intense series of lap dancing with botsies rooting laps like rotor rooters, frontwards and backwards. And hear Harrywills: "Down taw, nuh brush!" reminding us of the marble game where you were not allowed to remove any impediment between your marble and your opponent's or lift your knuckles to get an accurate shot.

Today both Harrywills and Harry's Nitery are gone. Now we have Viagra.

The Green Man in Trafalgar Square I

I BELIEVE that most people are familiar with the verb 'to shanghai'. If not, check your Oxford dictionary. Shanghai is usually known as the name of a city in China, but it was also used as a verb meaning "to drug and ship as a sailor unconscious." Literally to kidnap and put to work on a ship bound for Shanghai.

Would it surprise you to know that there was a verb called "to barbadose" which meant the same thing except that people were kidnapped and shipped to Barbados? There was a time when poor white Englishmen and Irishmen were given enough liquor to get them drunk or they were waylaid on a dark street or in an alley and knocked unconscious. Whichever method was used, these poor disenfranchised individuals used to end up on board a boat with other indentured men and women bound for Barbados.

By the time they arrived in Barbados they were all defined as indentured labourers, sentenced to spend years working off their sentence on plantations for free. Many suffered the ignominy of their class, unable to escape the horrendous conditions of compulsory labour. A few escaped and made their way to the colonies in America, most settling around Charleston, South Carolina where seven of them became governors of that state. Many also became pirates. The others who remained in Barbados eked out an existence on the periphery of the plantation system.

With the enslavement of Africans, whatever usefulness these

poor whites had became so negligible that at one point the government (consisting primarily of plantation owners) was forced to establish special schools to train them in survival skills. Things were that bad.

There was a wide gap, socially and economically, between the owners of plantations in Barbados and those who performed the adjunct roles of bookkeeper, overseer, keyman, etc. There was no hope of ascendancy of poor whites to the level of ownership in the seventeenth, eighteenth or nineteenth centuries. The few poor whites who succeeded, as well as the few 'coloured' or black, did so because they were highly successful blacksmiths, wheelwrights or shipwrights, skilled professions which allowed for the accumulation of the necessary capital to bid for a few of the bankrupt plantations that became available from time to time. Or in the case of Trents, Roebuck, Four Hill and Joe's River bought by blacks with Panama money in the early part of the 20th Century.

Let me indicate something of great importance about Barbados. The presence of the plantation house in Barbados is unlike any in the Caribbean. This is so with respect to the number, the size and architecture. The owners of these great houses were resident in Barbados and therefore all of their wealth was in Barbados. They were not absentee landlords like those found in other islands.

Although they remained in sugar until after World War II, many began to leave Barbados around independence time. This is my estimate based on the content of the public auctions that took place in the late sixties and early seventies. The quantity and quality of the silver, crystal, and furniture that was disposed of was unprecedented. I was told that the better items were taken away and what was left were those items that were either too bulky or were inferior in quality to those which were taken. I had the opportunity of seeing a collection of these valuables that

Bowen, the auctioneer, had assembled and eventually took with him to Miami.

It was this group who saw the value in Nelson's victory at Trafalgar. It was this group who feared what had happened in Haiti in 1791 and who were jittery about being outnumbered by blacks. It was this group who had marginalized the poor whites in St. John, St. Phillip, St. Joseph and St. Andrew. It was this group that had organized the Barbados Mutual Assurance Society to protect them from the vagaries of tropical hurricanes and the tempestuousness of British merchants. It was this group who set up the Court of Chancery to protect and control the sale of failed plantations in order to maintain control.

The twentieth century saw a weakening of this group as the few sons who survived both World Wars I and II had shifted their focus to the merchant business in Bridgetown. This change provided opportunities for poor whites to move up the ladder to managerial positions on the plantation. By the middle of this century many who moved to Bridgetown, living on Chapman Street, King's Street, Gill's Road and Baxter's Road, got opportunities to work as cash boys and clerks.

In other words, the majority of those who own and operate plantations today are not of that plantocratic class that was so thankful to Nelson. Indeed, those who are the shakers and movers in the business class are also not of that grouping either. Many of today's very successful white businessmen are from that lot of poor whites; those indentured servants who historically were despised by the plantocracy in the same way blacks were by the whole of white society. There was a pecking order.

As a matter of fact, most of the successful white businessmen gained their successes after this plantocratic group left the scene and after adult suffrage, which they fought against, and after independence when most of them abandoned the country.

It is therefore a conundrum to me that people who suffered historically at the hands of this plantocratic group (e.g. their treatment of both the Williams and Goddard families) should identify so strongly with Nelson and his position of preeminence. Is it because Nelson was white or green? Or is there another reason?

The Green Man in Trafalgar Square II

WHEN FORMER Prime Minister Erskine Sandiford wanted to put vendors in Trafalgar Square, I objected very strongly on my call-in program. The Barbados National Trust also objected and vigorously campaigned against the proposal. The time when this should be an area of commercial activity has long passed.

Whether as the Green or as Trafalgar Square or as National Heroes Square, this area has always been the psychological centre of the nation. Black people may have been submissive in their acceptance of its past significance, and it must clearly be understood that this evolution is natural and predictable.

I remember when this area served as the major bus stand for the island and always had a woogla of hawkers and vendors all around. In addition, donkey carts, dray carts, mule carts, luncheon carts, lumber carts, box carts of all descriptions, lorries and other vehicles used the area. And since the swing bridge swung in those days, the inner basin of the Careenage was always fully populated with inter-island schooners and the traders that emanated from this

ERSKINE SANDIFORD

activity.

In the last fifty years, changes in the economy and development of the country have forced a reconsideration of the use of Heroes Square. As Bridgetown expanded to the suburbs and to the residential areas in and about the city centre, and with the development of the deep water harbour, Heroes Square has evolved more and more as an area of national significance to complement the extended use of the parliament buildings by the legislature.

Vendors were removed from the Green (as opposed to the Lower Green at the other end of Broad Street) and the mouths of alleyways and given their own central markets at Cheapside and Fairchild Street. What is left now are the taxis whose time has come for relocation elsewhere. This means that the taxis must go.

National Heroes Square is about the reconstruction of ourselves with the intent of reinforcing the development of a national consciousness. The mere fact that this little island was discovered and settled by a European colonial power who occupied it for about three hundred and forty years cannot justify a perpetual adherence to that historical fact. The future has many more years ahead than the finite ones of colonial occupation.

We have inherited a language to which we have imposed our own vocabulary and grammar. We have inherited an education system and we have altered it to meet our own demands. Yet, in spite of our achievements, we are caught in a vicious eddy of racism that continues to define us according to the colour of our skin, the supposed inferiority of our managerial skills, our governance, our religions, our habits, our dances, and our music among other things.

If we question our disenfranchisement when it comes to the economic arena, we are defined as racists. If we question the use of nepotism as a means of keeping public companies in the control of whites, we are defined as racists. If we question the use of insurance funds, pension funds, National Insurance funds to prop up public companies, we are called racists. If we demand accountability of the same public companies, we are deemed racists.

If the way in which land is distributed and owned is questioned, you are accused of being anti-white. If you look at certain private firms and note that only certain people have all the jobs at the top, you are told that it is a private firm and that you can't tell them who to hire. For articulating this obvious fact that everybody can see, you are called a racist.

If you question the absence of certain people at the emancipation celebrations, you are accused of introducing race. If you select National Heroes and omit a white person, you are deemed to be racists. If you want to rename a National Park, it is deemed racist. If you want to move Nelson and replace him with the most significant figure in our political history, it is considered racist.

Thirty-three years after political Independence, a government of Barbados has decided to create for the nation run by the children of ex-slaves, a psychological centre of dominance. This has been a four-step process to bolster the self-confidence of our people.

The first was in two parts—the cautious and tentative erecting of a statue to emancipation and then the giving of full flower to recognizing Emancipation Day again.

The second was to recognize those who rejected the starvation, poverty and inhuman treatment meted out to them one hundred years after emancipation by recognizing their contribution with a Day of Significance, pardons, and erecting a bust to their leader, Clement Payne.

The third was to recognize those who contributed to the

CLEMENT PAYNE

development of the nation and the development of our people. Hence ten of the most outstanding persons were inducted into the pantheon of National Heroes and into our collective consciousness.

The fourth was to redefine Trafalgar Square and establish our presence, our psychological dominance at the centre of our nation. Therefore Nelson, the former Green Man of Trafalgar Square, had to go. You can't change the name of the Square and keep the image responsible for it.

I wonder why it is felt that the renaming of the square is for sale? Is it seen as just another plantation for sale? Is that racist?

The Black Man in Heroes' Square

THE CLAIMING of Trafalgar Square to establish National Heroes Square is a timely and fitting end to this millenium and this century. It is a controversial decision only for those who do not understand or are unwilling to accept the connectivity between the past and the future.

If we were to total up all the place-names in Barbados, it is more than likely that less than ten percent are named after black Bajans and few if any after places in Africa. It is only within the last thirty years that there has been a number of schools, streets, highways, roundabouts, buildings and places named after black Bajans.

Ironically, if you look at some of the old place names, especially plantation names, you will find that they too had other names over the period of their existence since a lot of these plantations were named after their owners. There is nothing sacrosanct about names. Naming is a significant process to those who do the naming and there is nothing stopping future generations from establishing their own names based on contemporary demands.

John Connell has eruditely demonstrated the way in which England dealt with its colonial past as an outpost of the Roman Empire. It renamed those Roman names with Anglo-Saxon names. The Iberian peninsula, Spain and Portugal, was under the rule of Islam for ten centuries and has been redefining itself since then.

Dr. Richard Allsopp has indicated that the word Bim has its

origins in Africa. He has suggested that it meant "our people." White Bajans co-opted the word to imply that Barbados was another English county with the name of BIMshire, which although it has appropriateness for us a nation, suggested a special characteristic about white Bajans. A siege mentality!

But it is not white Bajans only that seem to object to the process of renaming oneself and one's nation. There is a substantial body of black Bajans whose consciousness is so thoroughly indoctrinated by the dominance of European cultural expression and concepts of superiority that they are blinded to their own potential, in the past, the present and whatever future they have.

I have heard it said: "A whuh duh wan move Nelson fuh? I does pass dey and don't even kno dat he dey." Blinded or a negation of everything that they believed in their lifetime. To acknowledge the need for National Heroes Square and the new presence of a black man in National Heroes Square is too much to take. It is like saying to themselves that they failed, that they could have done better, that they could have asserted themselves and built this nation positively instead of succumbing to the dominance of the past. Their comfort zone and accustomed views are now challenged. The man in the mirror now looks like them. The man in the square is them.

It is easy to avoid making the intellectual leap to give sustenance and support to the assertion and maturation of the black presence in Barbados. But this leap is a problem for those who literally do not want to be dominated by blacks and by those who don't want to integrate into a system based on merit and ability.

Although a fillip has been given by the creation of a psychological dominance, it must not be seen as a racist response as some are wont to do, but be viewed as an assertion to counterbalance the persistent psychological battering given to the people of the African Diaspora by an international Eurocentric print and video culture.

It is not enough, however, to let this be the end all of black achievement. The economic enfranchisement must be the next task on the agenda. Corporations doing business with government and its agencies must reflect more closely the makeup of the nation. This must apply to both black and white companies. Public corporations must become more transparent and must not be used as a personal fiefdom of senior management.

Most public companies have investments emanating from National Insurance, from pension funds, from insurance premiums, and from credit unions. The majority of these funds come from the majority of people living in Barbados. The representatives of these funds must therefore ensure that these public companies have employment practices and policies that are transparent and fair. They must also guarantee that contracts for service also meet the same criteria.

Failure by the government to pursue economic enfranchisement and failure of public and private companies to be fair and provide opportunities to Bajans based on merit and ability will create a climate that can and will cause considerable pain to all.

Perceptions confirmed by visible inequities is a recipe for disaster. We have a square and must have a plantation too.

The Pride of Barbados

RUPERT YARDE was a mason who lived at the top of Hothersal Turning going up to Lears Gap. He was a man who loved his waters and always had a three-gill bottle stashed deep in one of his pants pockets. He was also a stick-licker who used to pelt bois with men from Trinidad.

RUPERT YARDE

Rupert Yarde was a soft stone mason, a man who worked building houses with twelve by twenty-four inch coral stone blocks. Sometimes the blocks were bigger, twenty-four by twenty-four, and had to be cut and trimmed. He marked a straight purple line with a sliver of wallaba wood dampened on the flat of his tongue.

Rupert Yarde and a next man would use in tandem a long saw with handles at each end to slice the soft stone in two. Sometimes they would use their blacksmith-made stone hammers. These hammers were shaped like tall Xs, one end tapered to a cutting edge and the other blunt for tamping and setting the stone.

Cutting stone in tandem from alternate sides was like hearing ancestral rhythms on a logdrum. As they cut, the two hammers set up a rhythm; each cut was an accented downbeat while the tamping side offered the softer beat on the side of the stone. And somewhere in between there was a ringing singing sound of steel when the hammer encountered a piece of conch shell or some other hardened stone, all the while each hammer twirling like a drumstick in the hands of a jazz drummer like Max Roach.

The walls of most of the buildings at Harrison College are made of these large coral stone blocks. The older buildings, like the Parliament buildings, stand naked and unplastered, blackened by age, their structure delineated for all to see. The other buildings are more sedately attired with mortared walls.

As a school boy sitting in these buildings, I often wondered if the builders of these magnificent edifices were like Rupert Yarde. Rupert Yarde and his assistants were the only masons I knew, just like how Professor Laha was the only joiner and magician I knew. Professor Laha built our dining room chairs and the tables and the couches and the bureau with the matching wardrobe and bed heads.

When Quick Step rang the bell to signal break or lunch, we made music on our desks and benches, searching assiduously for the right tones. Like the stone masons, we tapped ancestral rhythms, unacceptable Banja rhythms, culled in part from Tuk bands and calypsos.

Emile Straker and the Ward Twins, Lisle and Peircy, and my fledgling guitar vampings acquired from Jack Headley in a form or two above me were daring, unwelcomed explorations into our music. Only the sagacious Guess Box dared to go further and be a calypsonian. And there was Cedric Phillips and Maggie Goodridge who preceded us and scandalized the name and reputation of Harrison College by becoming real-real musicians and wasting "duh

EMILE STRAKER

fadda money."

On Sunday Night of August 2, 1998, at the Cohobblopot, at the Barbados National Stadium, in front a crowd of some 15,000 people one day after the celebration of Emancipation Day, Barbados honoured five outstanding Bajans for their creativity.

They were: Karl Broodhagen, George Lamming, Edward Kamau Brathwaite, Emile Straker and Anthony Gabby Carter.

These five brilliant story tellers have used music, sculpture and the word to tell us and the world about us: who we are, what we did, how we did it, where we came from. They have chronicled the known and the unknown. They have unravelled the mysteries of our past and the conundrums of our present. They are leaving us a profound knowledge and definitions of ourselves that will challenge generations to come.

These are ordinary men like Rupert Yarde, mason and stick-licker, and Professor Laha, joiner and magician. But they have signed their names on the coral stone corridors of time. They are immortal because our grandchildren and their grandchildren will know who they are. We recognize and honour them for their daring and their vision and their willingness to be different from the fowl, the fish and the red herrings.

It is a privilege to know them all. They are the Pride of Barbados.

Frothing Pee: the Environment and Community

Peter Must Help Pay For Paul

WHEN THE Emancipation Proclamation was introduced in 1834, African peoples of the Caribbean found themselves free but without land or shelter. The planters, on the other hand, faced the bleak prospects of not having any labour to work their fields or manufacture their sugar.

The planters were compensated by the British government and the Emancipation exercise was allowed to linger for four years, keeping the Africans from vacating the plantation under a so-called apprenticeship scheme. In other words, the planters were given time to protect themselves while ostensibly suggesting that this was for the benefit of preparing Africans for freedom. Freedom my eye!

In Jamaica, where there existed large tracts of Crown lands and abandoned plantation lands, freed Africans left the plantations and established free villages in abundance across the island on both private and Crown lands. From emancipation this concept of capturing lands became part of Jamaican cultural tradition.

In Barbados, there were no Crown lands, so freed Africans faced the dismal prospects of having to rent land from sympathetic land owners or sell their services to the highest bidder. To protect themselves from having to bid to get the labour of these new freed men, the government of Barbados (made up entirely of planters) enacted legislation which restricted the freed men from living on one plantation and selling their labour to another.

For example, most of the freed men lived in nigger yards. A

more respectable name is plantation tenantries. These tenantries were part of the plantation during slavery. It was on these lands that the Africans developed their little agricultural plots, built their homes and established their families.

Since they were no longer maintained by the plantation, they looked forward to working wherever work was available. This could mean plantations nearby or plantations farther afield.

However, the *Located Labourers Act* prevented such movement of freedmen. The plantation managers or owners had the right to remove them summarily from the nigger yard if they dared to work at another plantation while living on theirs.

This forced many workers to remain where they were and work for little or nothing at all until the Barbados Workers Union was formed. At about the same time in the early forties, the *Located Labourers Act* and the one related to the Third Gang (employment of children) were removed from the books.

There were a few urban tenantries existing at the time and these were overcrowded. Sanitation was non-existent and the health of residents was affected. Besides the usual diseases there were skin eczemas that caused what Bajans called 'poxy-ness'. It was such an unusual situation in the middle of this century to find people without a poxy foot or poxy face that the term 'clear-skin' was used to describe them.

I have never heard the word tenantry used in Jamaica, but you can find an abundance of squatters in the hills all over Jamaica on government (formerly Crown) and privately-owned lands. Only recently has the government began to deal with the rapid expansion of urban squatting and the capturing of land by people in need of housing. Unlike Barbados, elaborate wall houses are erected on these captured lands and this makes it difficult for private owners or government to remove them.

Urban squatting has serious consequences for public health in

Jamaica. For example, along the hillsides above the Hope River which feeds the Mona Dam you can find hundreds of illegal settlements with no access to running water or sewage systems or roads. But people don't see these problems. They feel that nothing has been done for them since slavery.

It was therefore surprising to see that Barbados has a developing problem with squatters. There was the Belle problem a decade ago and now Fairy Valley. What was interesting was hearing sentiments similar to those I heard in Jamaica.

What is clear is that we in the Caribbean cannot and must not forget what fate did to us during and after slavery. Although we have moved with alacrity into the twentieth century, upgrading the quality of life and providing education for people, we must remember that our governments have a responsibility to provide those of us who are in need with access to land or adequate shelter.

If Peter paying high taxes for a piece of this rock, then some of that should go to help Paul with his two-by-four lot.

We must never forget what happened to us at emancipation. Nor should we forget what happened to us in slavery.

Rockstones and Cement Blocks

THE BULLDOZER lowered its front-end like a Jamaican Red Poll bull-cow and took its aim at the neat little house with the akee tree and the lime tree at the side. The woman watched absent-mindedly while she listened to the ranting and raving of the community over these impending imperious actions calculated to remove all the houses in the area.

The land was needed by a real estate developer.

Like the sun bursting out of the night, it suddenly dawned on the woman that it was her house that was under attack by this heretic demolition squad. "Oh God," she screamed hysterically, "Oh God, don't kill meh pickneys," as she ran tumbling forward, scampering on both hands and feet, in front the bulldozer which had stopped as abruptly as it had started.

In a flash, she entered and exited the house with two little pre-school children under her arms.

The boisterous crowd that was dumbstruck into a frigid silence of inaction rapidly enveloped the woman and her children. What was just talk suddenly turned into an offensive war of rockstones. There was no shortage of ammunition. This part of the St. Thomas countryside is noted for its abundance of surface stones. Only the guttaperks were missing!

The parish of St. Thomas is noted for its rebelliousness. In 1865, there was an uprising in the parish capital of Morant Bay.

"Known as the Morant Bay Rebellion and led by Paul Bogle, it resulted in the killing of a number of whites. The uprising was put down by Governor Eyre with great severity. More than 430 persons were executed or shot, hundreds more were flogged, and 1,000 dwellings were destroyed. Bogle and George William Gordon, a prominent mulatto legislator of the day, were hanged. A century later, both Bogle and Gordon were declared national heroes."

I wrote some time ago that Jamaica was beset by squatting, particularly after emancipation when many a plantation was abandoned. It is also important to note that even today, many people do not have title to land. However, the occupied land is known as seed land—land that is passed from one generation to the next. And incidentally, the ancestors of many families are buried on these plots.

According to a spokesman for the community, these lands were in their possession for at least three generations. The community had approached several politicians (from both the PNP and the JLP) over the years to assist them in buying the land. The late Prime Minister, Michael Manley, is alleged to have tried to find

URBAN TENANTRY IN BARBADOS

the original owners or their descendants overseas. Nothing came of it.

Barbados never really had a problem with squatting as there was little land available. However, Barbados did develop a tenantry system that evolved from the nigger yards of slavery times. Up until the 1960s, owners of these tenantry lands could evict their tenants without notice and as callously as is being done to this community in Jamaica.

When President Kennedy Drive was built, it opened a lot of land that was used as tenantries, namely Rotten Town, Alkins Land, and so on. The owners of these lands immediately started to eject their tenants in order to capitalize on the access to the new road.

At the suggestion of the then Mayor of Bridgetown, Ernest Deighton Mottley, Errol Barrow introduced a *Tenantry Act* that defined a tenantry as having five or more tenants. Even this led to problems and the Tom Adams government reduced this definition to mean two or more tenants.

In order to upgrade these tenantries and protect the rights of the people who have been living there for at least five or six generations, recent governments have embarked on a program of upgrading the roads and services in the tenantries. The tenants can then purchase their lots at ten cents a square foot.

There is no such law in Jamaica and many families are not protected. The new owners of the property in question went to court to get title to the land. Their action in destroying the houses of the tenants was as callous an action as that of Governor Eyre in 1865. The demolition squad was alleged to have been spearheaded by gunmen whose role was to intimidate the residents. The action was unilateral and unnecessary.

The irony of the situation is that the land occupied by the residents is but a small fraction of what was acquired. However, it is in a prime location.

Kendall Plantation in St. John, Barbados, also has a tenantry. Somebody wants the tenants to leave because they are on prime land. I hope that bulldozers, like Jamaican Red Poll bull-cows, are not used to get rid of them.

Jamaica had Bogle and Gordon. Barbados had before them Bussa and Franklyn. Jamaica got rockstones, Barbados got cement blocks.

Frothing Pee: the Environment and Community

SETTING ASIDE the political disagreements about Independence, it was a great feeling to know that as a country we were free. But gnawing at my craw was the question of who I was. What made me a Bajan? I had already been tackling the question of my blackness, my Africaness, and trying to put that in a context of Barbados, the Caribbean and the World.

What makes me a Bajan? To answer that question I decided to talk to as many Bajans as possible. For five years I travelled to every nook and cranny in Barbados visiting and talking to people and recording some of the conversations on tape. At present, I am transcribing some of these conversations for publication and re-recording songs for a CD recording of Bajan folk songs.

There are two aspects to these investigations. First I travelled every single paved road in Barbados including those in new developments. I also covered about 60 percent of the cart roads, particularly those that offered me short cuts to various villages.

Physically, I found Barbados a fascinating place. I searched for Amerindian artifacts on the cliffs of St. Lucy, discovering in the process that cane used to be planted on these rocky grounds. I searched for horsenicker seeds and found trees on the beach by the Lazaretto and another set near Archers Bay, St. Lucy.

I followed the train line along the East Coast—Cattle Wash, Bathsheba, Tent Bay, Congo Bay, Bath, Consett Bay, Milady's Passage. All of this because I was told that Brumley's Brass Band used to play for excursions on the train. I didn't know Brumley, but I met a man in Welchtown, St. Peter who had a Brass Band playing jazz in the 1920s in Barbados too.

I stomped through gullies looking for hiding places where our ancestors could hide if they ran away from slavery. I found Coffee Gully down behind Castle Grant, damp and forlorn and magnificent in its beauty, only to discover that vandals were felling the hundred-foot tall coconut trees just to get a few coconuts.

Near Green's, St. George, I found the ruins of a factory built by a man called Adamstraw. At Roebuck, St. Peter, I studied the old factory purchased by Bajans who went to work on the Panama Canal. I stopped at every blacksmith shop to discover the secret behind the fabulous ironwork found in the donkey cart design.

I went down in quarries from Grazettes and Bush Hall in St. Michael to Chapel and Kirton's in St. Phillip to find masons who played rhythms with their blacksmith-made tools. These hammers used to ring when two masons in tandem cut and chipped and shaped the soft-stones blocks. I discovered Blackman's Bridge with its soft-stone arches behind Grantley Adams School on the cart road leading to what was then one of the most isolated villages in Barbados.

In all of these areas there were people who had stories to tell, people who had a profound interest in their community, an interest in setting standards for the whole community, taking care of and nurturing the future generation.

Older villages and communities were stable, predictable and were in existence for at least two or three generations. Over the years we have seen the development of numerous new villages and communities. Not much thought was given to the making of a community (except for the removal of residents from Chapman Lane/Emmerton to Clapham).

In newer developments, settlement takes place over a period of time and vagaries of human nature prevent mature adults from bonding immediately. But the opposite is true with children. It is they who establish the community, who learn it from inside out, who create it and know it. In the natural course of things, this takes a generation to mature. There is no reason why this should be left to fate. We need to use all the techniques available to assist communities to develop the cohesiveness that was the hallmark of our older communities. We need to reinvent communities.

For this reason, non-formal education techniques need to be brought to the forefront in cultural planning. We have seen the importance of preventive medicine to Caribbean communities. By instituting public health measures and through careful planning we basically removed most of the diseases that were wreaking havoc on our communities sixty years ago. Should we not do the same now for our environmental and psychological well-being?

We must begin as a people to rediscover our physical environment. We must share a sense of pride about this environment. To do so, we must be educated by those who know it. We must not just exist, we must recognize it as a major factor in our own personal survival as a person, as a family and as a people, as a nation.

The challenge is for us to see us, ourselves, at the centre of the world, with values worth preserving and enhancing. These perspectives should be incorporated in Mathematics and English and Geography and History and Science text books.

However, at the community level, we need to explore the meaning of community and develop new ideas to provide systemic and meaningful rites of passage for young people. Boys in particular need to know the rules of moving from boyhood to manhood. They can no longer depend on their pee frothing to know that they are expected to behave like men.

We must not take things for granted and assume that all will remain well.

Reinventing the Community 1

I BELIEVE it was Oliver Jackman who first made me aware that our neighbours were not only those who lived next to us, but those who we could reach on the telephone.

OLIVER JACKMAN

I am old enough to remember a Barbados where your neighbour was the person next door who you interacted with on a daily basis. It was you and your neighbours who formed a community.

This community was controlled by elders who had a collective responsibility over the young of the community. It was imperative that you respected these elders, else you paid the penalty when you reached home. And the information used to get home before you.

There were clear, defined rites of passage that permitted an orderly evolution from child to adulthood. These rites were demarcated by symbols or rituals (e.g., short pants to long pants, long pants to suit, confirmation, matinee to eight-thirty) to allow you to move from one point to another. If you tried to move upward too fast, you were quickly put in your place with some reminder about force-ripeness.

In the beginning, radio and later television did not create the pockets of isolation that they do now. As a matter of fact they were cohesive forces that brought people together to listen to the world news, and the fights, especially those of Joe Louis.

Today, satellite television and the internet continue to undermine the development of contiguous physical neighbourhoods.

There was also a time when communities were replete with members of the extended family living adjacent or within the same household or on the same compound. Employment was within the household or on the neighbouring ground so that adults were always near to their homes or easily accessible.

Today many persons have moved away from that extended family to establish homes in new developments. Often, it is the children who through their interaction will build the new community. When both parents and the single parent is working, many of these children are left to fend for themselves and in the absence of community controls find themselves in trouble more often than not.

There was also a time when the Church (all denominations) had a captive audience because it was the only entertainment around. The Church was organized: church services, Sunday school, bible classes, church army meetings, confirmation classes, church fairs, and so on.

People reacted with each other according to age groups, and it was not unusual to see the elders looking out their windows while chatting with other adults who were strolling around the neighbourhood. The children played games or told stories to each other in their groups until night closed in.

Today we call that lyming.

Besides these things there was a hand-me-down-knowledge of the environment and the plants about. These plants served as medicines and food for people, and as meat (feed) for animals. There were bushes for scrubbing and bathing of humans as well as animals.

There was community knowledge of animal husbandry. Mating seasons were known to all and sundry. One learnt how to use ashes to remove a pip from a fowl-cock's tongue or how to barrow a boar or where to stake out a cow, a sheep or a goat. Each had his/her own tastes.

Indigenous organizations like the Barbados Landship Movement, Friendly Societies like the CIVIC, social activities like Tea meetings, Service-a-songs and Singings linked one community to the next.

The educational system provided us with a profound understanding of the three Rs. We must also never forget that schools through the teachers in the system, conveyed knowledge of public and personal health, major community concerns that halted the debilitating spread of diseases in the community. How many chigoes were picked from barefoot boys and girls and how many lice were combed from natty dreads?

There are many more observations I could make about communities, but the essential point I want to make about the above is that in spite of the lack of modernization as we know it, there were things to do. There were controls, casually applied; values inculcated through daily and routine responsibilities; cooperation through games; and ethics from the church and the Anancy stories.

Today, communities exist as by definition they are. But how much is the interplay within these communities driven by people-to-people relationships as opposed to peer group relationships? How much is learnt that is based on morality and ethics? How much of the knowledge within a community is shared with all the members of that community?

I do not want to ignore the presence of technology that alters the way in which we react to each other. What I would like to see is that we use this same technology to reinvent communities, to assist us in arriving at an ideal, to balance and counteract further dislocation through cellular individualism.

It is neither a difficult nor formidable task. All the elements exist. All we need is the will.

Reinventing the Community 2

THE ANGLICAN Church has finally come around to believing that they are part of the solution to the many problems in Barbados. I am referring to Project Ploughshares.

First I must congratulate Rev. Jeffrey Gibson, rector of St. Leonard's Anglican Church and the Social Responsibility Commission which he heads, for devising this seven-week program to attack the scourge of violence that is so rampant in Barbados.

Project Ploughshares will operate on two fronts: the first is to focus on the sources and causes of violence using sermons with "such topics as anger, greed, jealousy, and drug addiction" and secondly, "community outreach programs and a nine-day cycle of prayer involving all denominations for peace in the nation."

The Anglican Church cannot be serious. The first part of Project Ploughshares is directed at its captive audience on Sundays and whenever, and those who come within the purview of those sermons in or about those churches or hear the occasional sermon on radio. As usual the Anglican Church is speaking to the converted.

The second part of "community outreach programs" has not been specified in the reports I've read, but I venture to state that I am suspicious of any program lasting for seven weeks that expects to solve an endemic problem such as violence in the community in such a short period of time.

I have said it, and I will say again and again that the question of tackling the social problems of Barbados can only be solved by tackling on an ongoing basis the non-formal learning that is taking place in the community at large. It has to relate to the environment, be functional, provide rites of passage and fill in for absentee parents.

I do not conceive of the Anglican Church and its associates in Christendom as being the priests. The Church must include those who are part of the captive audience on Sundays—those who are genuine worshippers who keep the faith, and those who come for the show.

So defined, the Church has at its beck and call a considerable pool of resourceful people covering every spectrum of human endeavour in this country. Journalists and media workers, artisans, teachers, hotel workers, sanitation workers, engineers, architects, doctors, sportsmen, and sportswomen, fishermen, taxi drivers, artists, musicians, et al. All of these people have knowledge to share and should be encouraged to do so. There is an old African proverb: "It takes a whole village to raise a child."

Why must the responsibility only be on the shoulders of the turn-collar men and women? This large congregation of worshippers and believers who are also deeply concerned with the deteriorating social situations must be willing to donate fifty hours (minimum) a year to share their knowledge with young boys and girls on the block—the lymers in limbo; especially the boys.

Another thing, aren't we supposed to be our brother's keeper? The Anglican Church, (and the Moravian and the Methodists), have all retrieved their property from government after a hundred years or so. Not one of the churches has been able to devise a modular program that can be used in these centres to salvage our young people from the brink of despair and disaster. Not one plan has been put in place to utilize these buildings as centres of learning sponsored by the church as a community for the community.

> ... it is not enough
> it is not enough to be free
> of the whips, principalities and powers,
> where is your kingdom of the Word?
>   ...
>
>
> I
> must be given words to shape my name
> to the syllables of trees
>
> I
> must be given words to refashion futures
> like a healer's hand
>
> I must be given words so that the bees
> in my blood's buzzing brain of memory
>
> will make flowers, will make flocks of birds,
> will make sky, will make heaven,
>
> the heaven open to the thunder-stone and the
> olcano and
> the unfolding land

Edward Kamau Brathwaite

No, Rev. Gibson, we are in need of something more profound and meaningful than sermons from the pulpit. That's a one-way street. That's like a radio or TV with the hope that you will have the same influence. Radio and TV are more pervasive. When you are, you may get the same result.

But the converted is not the problem. How do you bring the community into the church and how do you carry the church into the community? You need to create new situations for a sharing of information, knowledge and wisdom.

Take the catchment area of St. Leonard's. How do young people cope with homework, with drugs, with overcrowding, with hunger? What are the value systems that influence their day-to-day lives? Who are their mentors, their guides, their pilots through the catacombs of life? Who gives them dreams of tomorrow?

We print elaborate books [*Insight Guide to Barbados*, 1986 Edition or *Ins and Outs of Barbados*, 1998] to inform visitors about us and our country. Very few of us use these books to inform ourselves about us. And that can't be right.

I congratulate you on the initiative, Rev. Gibson, even though I don't know or understand the meaning of the word 'ploughshare'. And when you propose nine days of prayer, I remember the crop season evangelists who used to pray from January to June; that is, when Crop Season is on and workers have money in their pockets and are able to keep the coffers of the evangelist filled.

The world may have been made in seven days, but seven weeks can't remake a community. But as they say in Jamaica, wheel and come again. I know the Anglican Church and the churches in general can do better than that. You have to.

Reinventing the Community 3

ADAMSTRAW RUINS are found just outside of Greens, St. George, just after you pass Drax Hall Great House on your way to St. John. It is not a large compound, less than an acre, and before the trees and shrubs took hold, you were able to enter the building and explore the huge rooms above and below the ground.

The walls are about three feet wide and are made of huge coral stone blocks, exquisitely laid and finished. Adjacent to the building is also the ruin of an old mill wall. This mill wall is smaller than the usual sugar mill walls and appears to have been used to pump water.

I believe that Adamstraw was an artisan. I know that he was related to Justice Frederick Waterman and perhaps his cousins Justices Denys and Colin Williams, to former Judge Sir Frederick (Sleepy) Smith and all the Smiths, to Robert Best, former Editor of the *Advocate* and his brother, former Chief Meteorological Officer Deighton Best.

FREDERICK WATERMAN

This vacant ground, this vacant little pasture between the road and the buildings of Adamstraw Ruins, served as a playing field for the youth of Greens. The present owners are unknown. Several years ago Louis Tull and I tried to find the owners with little success. They had migrated to the UK.

Greens, like several other communities across Barbados, fell outside the ambit of the official Community Centres afforded by the various governments of Barbados. There are maybe fifteen or more centres developed over the last fifty years when community development was considered a valid tool for expanding the skills and knowledge of people.

All across Barbados, people have conscripted (or captured?) pieces of land to make cricket or football grounds or netball courts. Even smaller spaces are used for basketball dunking. In many cases though, these have been established with the help of plantations owners or government. These were not conscious decisions of the Community Development, Sports Council or Cultural Departments of government, but invariably through the initiatives of the people within the community.

Where government has provided facilities for sports, these have concentrated on cricket and football, lawn tennis and basketball/netball at or near the existing community centres. And the glaring failure of these decisions was that the grounds were always open and unfenced and coaches were never provided in any meaningful way to fully make use of the non-cricket/football facilities.

The absence of grounds with secure facilities—like Empire, Wanderers or Carlton grounds—prohibits the local communities from being able to use these facilities for fund-raising and more importantly, for developing semi-professional sports.

There is a need for serious rethinking to provide across the country about ten floodlit mini-stadiums, each with seating for around 2,000. Such stadiums would allow communities to establish competitive team sports in basketball, netball, lawn tennis, paddle ball etc. which can be supported by the very people who attend these events. These would also give the national associations a chance to play a much larger role in developing a wider participation in their sports nationally.

At the same time, with proper design, these community mini-stadiums could meet the demands of the entertainment industry, providing small economic venues for performances in and about communities. This would certainly reduce the pressure on the local transport system. Communities would be in a position to become more self-sufficient and less dependent on government for continuous support.

As important as sports are to the physical and mental development of those who participate in them, there are other important aspects of development of the individual as well as the community as a group that needs facilities. Some of these facilities are community centres, but they are not accessible to the majority of communities.

Primary schools remain the major sites for community activities. But recent and continuing consolidation of the primary school system has removed some of them from immediate access by communities. These retired primary schools buildings, the ones handed back to the churches, should be used to strengthen the non-formal and informal system of education within communities.

Skills training programs have in the past destroyed the effective uses of some community centres for personal development programs. These programs were important, but because of the specific equipment placed at centres, the use of those centres was limited after that and was the cause of much conflict within the community. Some centres became tied to a particular craft and this resulted in persons being brought from all over the island for that particular program. This also added to the conflict and alienation of people in the community.

Skills training has never pursued alternative facilities such as old buses or containers converted into mobile workshops which could be taken from location to location as the program requires. Encouragement must be given to young people to develop their skills within their community, and to apply their training to help eliminate the needs within that community.

Several years ago, the then Barbados Industrial Development Corporation's (BIDC) Handicraft Division ran a program where they brought young people from all over the country to attend a variety of workshops at its headquarters at Pelican Village. These young people were given weekly grants to cover bus fare and lunch.

If a course ran for six, ten, or fifteen weeks, about two weeks before it ended, the young people were looking for jobs elsewhere in town. As a result, the training was for naught.

Two things were obviously happening. First, the young people were getting accustomed to getting up on mornings, dressing up, catching the bus like other workers and heading for town. Familiarity with town, networking with friends and fellow travellers and others in the world of business allowed them to identify other places of potential employment.

Secondly, the training was not connected to the community and the resources available in the community to develop specific crafts. The emphasis was on a job rather than on self-sufficiency.

Training and the development of consciousness of self and one's place in the environment is part of the exercise of reinventing the community. Such development must take place in the community.

Reinventing the Community 4

THE NORTH Eastern part of Barbados is a hostile environment. Barren, rocky soil and a blighting, corroding, salty wind that nyam metal like fire nyam cane trash.

Rockfield Community Centre in St. Lucy, by name and nature, sits in such a landscape. It is the centre for a diverse and scattered community whose past life was dependent on sugar. And except for a few rum shops and mechanical workshops, there is little economic activity to sustain the community. Most of the people in the area who worked, worked away from the community. Those who didn't, remained trapped like clumps of wild cane oblivious to the hostilities rent by the salt air.

David was the caretaker of the Rockfield Community Centre when I met him. Unfortunately, I cannot recall his last name now. He was upgraded to a Community Development Officer and encouraged to take a more active role in the community. Where he saw a need, he acted.

David, on his own initiative, contacted the Scout Headquarters and in no time established a Scout Troop of which he was the Scout Leader. This little troop responded well and its members were exposed to the basics of scouting and the inherent principles involved.

Scouting in Barbados has a long tradition and although its origins go deep into our colonial past, it offers Rites of Passage for young boys and girls in a structured process. The fact is that the Scout Movement has become a major international movement.

There are over 25 million scouts in 210 countries. Of these, two-thirds are in so-called developing countries. In so becoming, it has also absorbed national ideals and objectives.

The Scout Movement has grown considerably in scope from its origins in 1907. There are now four divisions of scouts: Beaver Scouts from 6-8 years, Cub Scouts from 8-10.5 years, Scouts from 10.5-15.5 years, and Venture Scouts from 15.5-20. I believe there is also a Sea Scouts division. The International Movement now caters to both boys and girls.

This organization, more so than any other, covers the very critical ages at which boys are or can be led astray. And although I am not going to claim any prophylactic absolutes for the Scout Movement to alter the attitudes of our youth, it is a major platform for reinventing communities and tackling future attitudes.

When one considers the value systems, the attitudes and practical accomplishments inculcated by the Scout Movement, we can see why it should become a major platform to tackle future violence, crime and delinquency.

It is said that most people learn approximately 11 percent of what they know by listening, but 83 percent of what they know by seeing (observing and reading). People recall 20 percent of what they have heard but can recall 50 percent of what they have both heard and seen. Scouting as a practical exercise should remove a considerable number of youth from the pernicious violence and short-term solutions of television.

The Scout Movement depends heavily on voluntary participation, both at the leadership and membership level. And although David in my example was able to become a Scout Leader as quickly as he did, I expect that some measure of training should be given to prospective leaders.

What David also proved is that leadership is accessible to anyone who desires to help a community develop and who wants to alter conditions around them. And why not? People are parents, church members, job holders, and so on. The majority of people in our communities are responsible people.

Such involvement will result in an expansion of the consciousness and responsibility of the community at large. This should help widen the numbers involved in planning the future of our youth. In essence, this is what is needed.

But it cannot be done without the comprehensive support of the Community Development Department, the National Cultural Foundation, the Youth Division and the government at large. The Scout Headquarters would need to be properly staffed and equipped, to have training programs funded, and to have access to community facilities.

Not all young people will join the scouts, and there are several other groups like the Girl Guides and the Church Brigade which need support. Also, there is the opportunity to develop our own indigenous grouping, the Landship Movement, to foster and retain our continuum of linkages with our heritage.

It is important that we begin to focus on our youth, particularly those between the ages of eight and eighteen. We need to divert youth energies and curiosities into areas of constructive development.

We cannot continue to ignore that social controls previously instituted by the village have become irrelevant because of more working and absentee parents, fractured extended families, confused curricula in schools, disinterested authority, incompetent religious leadership, joblessness, and uncaring communities.

We see the symptoms. Let us retrain ourselves with a vision of beneficial communities.

Water All Around and Not a Drop To Drink!

I DISCOVERED Bussa in early 1967 in a small booklet describing the enquiry into the 1816 slave revolt. The booklet was hidden behind some books in the library of the Barbados Museum.

I wrote down the names of the plantations listed in that booklet and set about visiting every one, systematically looking at the houses, the yards and the gullies around the plantations. I tried to get a feel for the distances and relationship of the places so that I could have a better understanding of the events as they unfolded that Easter in 1816.

At Byde Mill, I met an old man who took me up Featherbed Lane where I could look down on Byde Mill. He showed me Drax Hall Jump and Drax Hall Woods and other plantations on the flat. He showed me the gully coming from Kendal and showed me the wells that carried off the excess water. He also told me that he was told by his grandfather that there was a dam at the mouth of the gully.

The idea of dams surprised me, but I subsequently discovered that this was also the case in parts of St. Peter. A number of dams were built in St. Peter to collect water. How long they lasted, I don't know, but I was shown water marks and remnants of such a system.

Across Barbados, you used to find an extensive system of wells in the middle of cane fields, near roads, in bottoms. They were part of a drainage system developed by the erstwhile planters to protect their cane fields from flooding. They were also part of an ecological system that provided a breeding ground for frogs.

Then there were the wells found in the yards of many houses. No doubt some of these have been filled in or abandoned. Both my Aunt and my Grandmother who lived in Speightstown had wells that produced potable water. No wonder then that the Water Authority is asking people with wells to notify them so that the wells could be registered.

Modern cultivation methods and lack of foresight have led to many of the ponds being eliminated from cane fields. The water that was collected is now channelled seaward using the road network.

A case in point can be seen at Lower Burney, opposite the Shell gas station in Two Mile Hill. There is a playing field at Dash Valley. At the edge of that field, next to the road, was a substantial depression that collected water in the rainy season and slowly fed it into the underground aquifers.

Now someone is filling in this depression to extend the playing field and losing sight of its importance to the drainage and water system of Barbados. Two Mile Hill and Government Hill are now major conduits for taking rainwater into the sea.

There is an obvious need for coordination of public projects between the Water Authority and the Ministry of Public Works.

Some years ago, Herman Lowe invited me to go underground at Bowmanston and see the condition of the underground rivers. Unfortunately, I am not so bold. But his concern was the amount of garbage in the form of non-degradable plastic bags and other containers that inundated this underground river.

Some of these items are obviously getting into the drainage system through the indiscriminate dumping of garbage in gullies and what is assumed to be dry wells. These items are calculated to block the filtering system of the underground aquifers.

It was a shock to me to see Barbados mentioned in *The Economist* as one the ten worst countries in the world for the supply of potable water. This fact has now been emphasized by the decision of establish a desalination plant at Spring Garden. How ironic considering that Spring Garden got its name from the abundance of springs that were found in this area.

I think the time has come for us to establish a major conference on the environment in Barbados where all parties— the agriculturalists, the energy producers, the tourism sector, the water people, the chemical suppliers, et al.—must discuss and determine what the future needs of Barbados will be.

This conference is really about involving and informing the public. It is not enough for the technocrats to have this information; the public must also have access to it in order to alter their patterns of behaviour, in order to protect the future of our countries.

It is not a matter of too many golf courses or too much development or too much of this or of that. It is about having a well-informed population which can understand the consequences of its behaviour and the limits that are necessary to safeguard our existence

ELOMBE MOTTLEY

Blue Skies and Passovers

Blue Skies and Passovers

THERE IS a certain spot down below Bissex House on a little hill above the Water Works tank. There was a time that this hill was just a grassy knoll covered with sour grass, a few maypole trees and some scraggly iron-wood trees; some people call them river-tamarind. It was a useless spot for cultivating, as it was rocky. There was no doubt that in earlier times it was used for planting sugar, but wind and water erosion had bared its back causing it to be abandoned. It was known as rab land.

I used to spend many days sleeping on this little hill sheltered only by an Advocate on my face. Most times I used to sit and watch the blue blue skies and the playful scuds that raced across from the east. Sometimes they were fat and black and moved much slower bringing passover showers.

The sun would be shining bright bright and yet you would get these passovers, not enough to soak you, but enough to cool you off. Still you tried to find something to cover you, as they were still unpredictable. I used to recall the story about the devil and he wife fighting for the coo-coo stick.

At other times I used to watch the distant waves rolling in from Africa. I tried to hear the sounds of the rolling surf and the sounds of dolphins, to see if the wind could indeed carry them to me. Sometimes I heard the voices of all those who came before me, those who perished in the middle passage, those whose spirits wandered around in search of Guinea.

Perhaps if I said I did I would have ended up in Jenkins, as that was a time when to hear the voices of Africa meant you were a madman or a racist. It was a difficult time to see the obvious. Ignorance had so seized people that it was you who were in danger.

Yet, we were talking about Independence and could not see the forest for the trees. We could not see who we were. We discarded the Union Jack for the Broken Trident. The trident, a symbol of Poseidon/Neptune, of Greek/Roman European tradition. The broken trident was more a broken fork and our gardens remained uncultivated, our children remained unnurtured, without a sense of being, of who they were or who they wanted to become.

So passovers were a solace down below Bissex House where dreams were worked out to the accompaniment of the susurration of sour grasses and the imaginary rhythms of the sea.

Barbados has changed a lot since those days. Thirty-three years after Independence, we have the innovative politics of inclusion that has allowed those who dream of a different Barbados to play a role in formulating and effecting policy. No longer are differences castigated, discarded or marginalized, at least in theory, and one hopes that inclusion and respect will become the norm.

ERROL BARROW

What is obvious and is outside of the grasp of the members of the Democratic Labour Party is that Errol Barrow is now a National Hero, and not just a hero of the DLP and its supporters. This means that Barrow's achievements are not just those of the DLP, but those of the Nation and that means the Barbados Labour Party and its followers.

The Barbados Labour Party has put a closure to the

GRANTLEY
ADAMS

developments that started with the riots in 1937. Whatever were the driving forces and differences between Grantley Adams and the BLP and Errol Barrow and the DLP is now a matter of history. This is the start of a new era, the symbol of which is the new Republic.

There is with the new Republic a redefinition of self, of who we are. There is also a strong vision of who we are to become as a people, not based on past objectives, but on objectives of the future, that Barbados is capable of being a first world country.

OWEN ARTHUR

Several years ago when I was Director of the National Cultural Foundation, I had occasion to meet with Owen Arthur who was then a Minister of State in Prime Minister Tom Adams' office. Owen Arthur emphasized two things in our discussions: people and their culture, which together form the basis of all government activity, and management by objectives. Anyone reading the Barbados Labour Party's manifesto will see this. This vision says that people matter.

In the past, the world moved so slowly that one was fairly certain that objectives could be achieved at a leisurely pace without fear of contradiction except for those things wrought by God. Unfortunately, today, the changing pace of technology and the abundance of information call for a far more sophisticated management response.

As the new era begins, we are fortunate to have a government which has a defined vision, set objectives, but remains flexible

TOM ADAMS

115

enough to respond to shifting paradigms.

After 63 Years, Same Khaki Pants?

"It is still unfortunate that less than 30 per cent [of Barbadians] own property, and we have to look at that," (Minister of Housing, Gline) Clarke said. "That is why we want to ensure that our children and grandchildren in the next couple of years are given the right to own land."

Nation, Thursday, May 25, 2000

MINISTER GLINE Clarke stumped me when he claimed that less than 30 percent of Bajans own property. Is that 30 percent of 270,000 people or of the 75,000 plus homes in Barbados? Before I comment on this, let me take you back 63 years.

Monday, September 13, 1937. Day 18 of the enquiry into the "Barbados Disturbances" of 1937. The witness is a white Bajan, Mr. H. A. Cuke, Senior Partner of the firm of Bovell and Skeete, Auditors (forerunners to Coopers Lybrand, Barbados). The questioner is Mr. Erskine R. L. Ward, a lawyer.

Mr. Ward: But most of the places changing hands in the last ten years have been sold to people with big groups of estates...

Mr. Cuke: And some have been getting rid of them. I do not think you can say that, because land has been sold at a high price, that in itself is any criterion.

Mr. Ward: Then all of these people are only speculators?

Mr. Cuke:	You know Mr. Ward, as well as I do, that there is land hunger in this island and people are prepared to pay for land.
Mr. Ward:	It is not the land-hungry man, it is the businessman who is buying land at this high price.
Mr. Cuke:	We have admitted that people are paying too much for land.

The Commissioners, GC Deane, Chairman, ERL Ward and Mathew A. Murphy submitted their report on November 2, 1937. Sections 57 and 58 read as follows:

The most urgent need to our minds is the provision of houses not only for the working classes, but also for persons somewhat higher in the social scale. We are not unmindful of the outburst of activity in house building during the past three years, but, as far as we can judge, the majority of the houses recently constructed will have a rental value far beyond the means of the ordinary clerk or artisan. If these houses were suitable for occupation by persons who live in overcrowded areas, they would still be hopelessly inadequate to meet the needs of the situation.

We have visited some of the slum areas of Bridgetown and some of the tenantries in the suburbs, and we share the opinion of all impartial observers that these would be a disgrace to any community, however backward, and are a standing reproach to local apathy and inertia.

The Commissioner of Police complained also of the difficulty of patrolling areas like Golden Square and Suttle Street where policemen can be attacked from narrow and unlighted alleys. It appears to us to be imperative that these slum areas be cleared and we recommend that the houses in Golden Square and Suttle Street be either removed or demolished and the owners compensated, and that these areas be preserved as open spaces.

It is essential in our opinion that the drift into the congested areas around Bridgetown be checked, and to this end we recommend that no permission for the selling or letting of lands in spots for the establishment of tenantries be granted hereafter within a radius of two miles of Trafalgar Square.

It is clear that from the evidence given before us that house rent among the lower classes is a serious factor in the family budget and there can be no doubt that the rent is in some cases exorbitant. The opportunity to purchase a house and land by weekly payments in lieu of paying rent will be a boon which will be highly appreciated by artisans and labourers. The building of these houses will provide continuous employment for a number of carpenters and masons who now suffer from periodic employment.

This is what is said today. Senator Peggy Rickinson said there needed to be some transparency in the distribution of land in Barbados. She pointed out that exorbitant land prices were disadvantaging low-income earners who also had a right to own land, preventing them from becoming landowners and eventually homeowners [Nation].

Senator Sir John Stanley Goddard is concerned about the cost of land and building in Barbados.

He said an increasing number of Barbadians felt they were "unable to afford a piece of this rock." This, he said, was a very sensitive issue which needed to be addressed by government. "I'm hearing more and more concerns being expressed in this area of land ownership. And we have to find a solution because it's a serious social concern." [*Nation*]

What exactly does Minister Clarke mean? And what does his Prime Minister have to say after 63 years? Same khaki pants?

It is not enough, Mr. Prime Minister!

"If land came up for sale tomorrow and I had the money, I would buy it. Why not? I'm not telling you I would keep it. I would sell it if I could make money on it... I buy land because my mother, who was fiercely competitive, told me that anytime I get money, buy some land because it doesn't spoil and you can't go wrong. And I've never lost money on land, so why should I stop buying it? I don't buy it and keep it, I sell it."

C.O. Williams in an interview with Hayden Boyce, Nation,
July 19, 1999

WHO LOST money on land? Not Mr. Williams. Not Mr. Corbin. Not Mr. Pillersdorf. Not Mr. Ronald Tree. Not Mr. K.R. Hunte. Not Mr. George Clarke. Not Mr. and Mrs. Ram. Not Mr. Wilkie. Not Mr. Davis. Not Mr. Deane. Not Messrs. Manning. Not Mr. Darcy Scott. Not Mr. Joy Edwards. Not Mr. Alleyne.

Not anyone who gets permission for subdivision from the Town Planning Department or the Minister responsible for that department. The Prime Minister is in charge of that department. So maybe the Prime Minister should explain why building lots are not available for Black people in Barbados.

Minister Gline Clarke, Minister of Housing, has said there are over 10,000 applications for house spots, that is, land. Mr. Clarke certainly ent wake up one morning and find that 10,000 people arrived at that conclusion overnight. Does the Prime Minister have any idea how many applications are made to the Town Planning Department for subdivision of land and whether or not that department is releasing an appropriate number to meet the demand? If not, why not?

As I have pointed out in previous articles, this land thing is a funny business. No matter what Black people do they can't get access to land either as developers or buyers and when they do policy decisions go against them. If a crab try to get out of the bucket, some gun hold on to he foot and pull he back down. I never see nuhbody holding on pon Mr. Williams's foot. As a matter of fact, he does seem to get all the help he want. Don't mind how he like to keep nuff nuff noise, he was always like that. But then again, Malcolm X always said it is the squeaky hinge that does get the oil!

Three years ago when the building boom was taking place on the West Coast and artisans were flush with money, government was vacillating and indecisive about accepting initiatives from private developers. As a result the artisans and builders bought Japanese old iron (used cars). Mr. Clarke knows this. Yet, there was no indecisiveness about Westmoreland and Bennetts plantations and Sandy Lane. If one looks at the profile of other land developments in Barbados, Mr. C.O. Williams is like Lara, at the top or near the top. So it is not surprising to read Mr. Williams' statement above.

Mr. Williams is a speculator. Read his statement again. I would like to be like Mr. Williams. Every Black Bajan should aspire to be like Mr. Williams too. But unless they have a friend in the bank, they does 'get screw in a vertical position', first by the banks, then the bureaucracy and the politics of scarce resources.

Over a hundred years ago, in the last part of the eighteenth century, there was a Court of Chancery which used to block the sale of failed plantations on the open market. This Court was run by the big estate owners, the politicians of the day. So the few Black people who had money (blacksmiths, wheelwrights, shipwrights), had difficulty buying some of these plantations.

Sir Bernard St. John's grandfather, Miller Austin, was one who succeeded. He bought Malvern in St. John. The Black people who went to help dig the Panama Canal pooled their money (which they saved in the government Savings Bank) and bought Joe's River in St. Joseph, Trents in St. James, Four Hill and Roebuck in St. Peter.

For years, Trents, in the heart of the tourism sector in Holetown, could not be developed because it was in Zone 1 or 2. These are water zones. It was subdivided into several six acre lots ostensibly for agriculture. Errol Barrow and Olwyn Weekes were two of the owners of these lots. Dennis Tull purchased Mr. Weekes' lot and applied for subdivision. It was refused on the grounds that it was in a water zone. Westmoreland plantation butt and abound Mr. Tull's land. Westmoreland was given permission. Houses were supposedly built in Zone 2 and the golf course in Zone 1. How many Bajan developers have been given the option of putting in a sewage system? Was Bennetts the same?

Recently the same Mr. Olwyn Weekes has been speaking out about the so-called land shortage. This is what he had to say: "Stop crying that you do not have any land available to put people's houses on. That is a myth. All you need to do, Mr. Minister, is to go to every plantation and take off 100 acres. You do not need to go into the tenantries ... It is long overdue, and you would have all the land you want, but you must have the political will and the political desire to make the people in Barbados understand that you have to give up some to the people who have none."

> It is not
> it is not
> it is not enough
> it is not enough
> to be able to fly to Miami,
> structure skyscrapers,

excavate the moon-
scaped seashore sands to build hotels, casinos,
sepulchres.

Edward Kamau Brathwaite, *Negus*

It is not enough, Mr. Prime Minister, for Black people in Barbados to own less than 30 percent of their own land.

Whuh you gine do, Gline?

"Minister of Housing Gline Clarke said many people preferred to invest money in cars and other things instead of land."

Nation, Thursday, May 25, 2000

LAND OWNERSHIP in Barbados is a funny thing. I don't mean Ha Ha. This is serious. Black people in Barbados seem to forget that they descend from an institution in which they owned nothing. In fact they were owned from head to splayed toes, from headtie to foetus, generation after generation, that is, those who survived to produce progeny.

Black people worked this land from the inside out with hoe and fork, barefoot, from sunup to sundown, for over 300 years, without a red cent. And nearly twenty years after Bussa and he crew bust up the landowners tail and frighten the juices from them waist, Black people get them freedom. Emancipation. And not a red cent in backpay. Not even a spot of land.

Freedom to move, to go out and capture piece of land because, in Africa, the land belongs to those who can work it. Living on it was also seen as working it. Nearly all over the Western world where there were public lands, freed blacks instinctively developed settlements after emancipation (the USA is another story). Those who

GLINE CLARKE

125

opted for the towns and cities found themselves with nothing. Their only asset was their labour. In Barbados, there were no public or Crown lands, so Black people were locked to the plantation.

In Barbados, because that cheap labour was pure profit, laws (the *Located Labourers Act*) were enacted by the land owners to stop the newly freed Black people from selling their labour to the highest bidder while living on a particular plantation. And so Plantation tenantries developed. Some ran to town, rented a room or a spot of land to build a shack.

Over the years many areas in urban St. Michael absorbed the movement away from the plantation tenantry and evolved into urban tenantries: Carrington Village, Bannister Land, Hanschell Land, Alkins Land, Phillips Land, Bay Land, Water Hall Land, New Orleans, to name a few. And there are many more.

Government acquired some of these in the 1950s and provided better housing conditions (Bay Land). Some owners of urban tenantries subdivided the properties and sold them to tenants, (the Orleans), the smallest lot size was 2,400 sq. ft. moving in the last forty years to 3,000 sq. ft. The landowner was responsible for providing water, light and road.

In the early 1960s, President Kennedy Drive was built connecting Fontabelle to Eagle Hall bypassing the congested areas of Barbarees Hill/Baxter's Road/Milk Market/Tudor Street. This road cut through many of the densely populated smaller urban tenantries running from Holborn (ESSO) through to Hanschell Land passing through places like Rotten Town and other areas that shocked Rev. Joseph Atherley the other day.

Without hesitation, many of the tenantry owners gave their tenants a week's notice to move because President Kennedy Drive opened access to their land and created new opportunities. The social dislocation was going to be monumental and the Errol

Barrow government enacted legislation defining a tenantry as having seven or more rented spots of land. Tom Adams government reduced the number to five houses. As such a tenantry owner was restricted in removing his tenants from the land. Where on one hand it protected the tenants, it also acted as a disincentive to owners who abandoned any responsibility for the land.

In some cases government has had to assume responsibility for these tenantries. In the case of plantation tenantries, government has been buying these at ten cents a square foot from the plantations and putting in the required services and selling them to the tenants.

The first Barbados Labour Party government under Grantley Adams eased the demand for housing with housing solutions in the Pine, Grazettes, Deacons, Bay Land, Gall Hill (Ch. Ch.), Six Roads, Lammings, etc. The Democratic Labour Party also did their own solutions throughout the country. None of these houses nor the little, little piece of land they sit pon belong to these tenants. They cannot go to a bank and use that house and land as an asset and say "I own a little piece of this land. My navel string not only buried here, but I own a piece of this rock."

What Minister Gline Clarke is saying is that after living pon this rock for nearly 350 years, 70 percent of the people in Barbados (95 percent Black, more than 55,000 out of 80,000 households, more than 189,000 people out of a population of 270,000 people, or more than 88,000 people out of a working population of 125,000) do not own land or a house and can't get land to buy.

Why is it that Black people don't own property and prefer to buy cars and other things? Minister, do you and your Prime Minister have a solution? Whuh you gine do, Gline?

A Babb is not a Babb

NANCY AND Dick Sonnis were strangers; to me, but not to Barbados. They were from Boston, Massachussetts, USA. A cold and formal city spired in money. They lived part of the year in a villa on the eastern terrace of Sandy Lane Estate.

They wanted to talk art with us (me, Omowale Stewart and Beverly Lashley). They wanted to sponsor a prize to purchase art for a national collection. I wondered how they knew we were working on such an idea at the National Cultural Foundation (NCF). I was at the time seeking approval from my Board to register a company in Delaware in the USA. This company would have a number of prominent Americans and friends of Barbados on the Board. The concept was to provide a charitable institution in the USA that would receive gifts and allow the donors to deduct these gifts from their taxes. I was having difficulties with certain members of the NCF board, so it was fortuitous that the Sonisses called.

FIELDING BABB

The Sonnisses were collectors of art. Of Bajan art. If memory serves me right Fielding Babb was among the artists in the collection. I subsequently discovered that they had a very fine collection of the vernacular work of the mystical Joseph Griffith of Henry's Lane in Bridgetown.

The instructions to reach the villa were clear and precise. You travel down Holders

Hill, turn right by the big tree as if you going to John's Plain, pass the house with the model windmill in the yard, follow the road through the dairy farm, turn right then left until you see a next left turn that pass by a gully where people does dump the garbage. When you get to the intersection, keep to the right until you come to the house without a gate. That was the villa.

The villa was plumb centre of a well-manicured lawn bordered by hedges of assorted hibiscuses, bougainvillea, and sweet lime. A necklace of other flowering plants circled the soft-stone walls of the villa on the eastern side. On the west, an open patio provided a magnificent view of the sea. Below the patio, a ripple-less swimming pool sucked the colour from the sky.

Inside the villa, Fielding Babb's bold colours matched the gardens and the magnificent cloths of the upholstered chairs. The walls were literally littered with Bajan landscapes including Babb's. It was an appropriate setting to discuss art and consume chocolate brownies.

On leaving the Sonnises, I couldn't help but notice the beautiful field of golden sour grass, fenced by the impertinent and impervious kuss-kuss grass. I realized this was an old field. In the olden days when cane was planted in holes, kuss-kuss grass was used to keep topsoil from washing into the road. Only the excess water could get through.

It was the Sonnises' land. They purchased it as a single 50-acre lot in order to retain the vista up to the next ridge across the cow pastures to where Norwoods began. They didn't want any houses to be constructed above them. So they bought it from dairy farmer Victor Babb.

The first two farmers I knew as a boy were Sam Marshall, who ran a magnificent organic farm in the back of Eckstein Village on about fifteen acres of land, and Dan Springer, a dairy farmer who ran a dairy farm on about an acre of land in Jack-Muh-Nanny-

Gap (Wavell Avenue). Dan Springer depended on many little people to raise his calves since he didn't have access to land.

Victor Babb was fortunate. He started as a cowboy with Janet Kidd, the daughter of the late British newspaper magnate, Lord Beaverbrook, who established the dairy farm. When Mrs. Kidd decided to quit farming, she sold the dairy farm to Victor Babb.

Throughout the years, Victor Babb ran a modestly successful farm. He had well laid out fields of pangola and other special grasses, irrigation, tractors and other baling equipment, barns and so forth. He had a modern farm with potential.

Sometime in the eighties, Americans were producing so much milk that in order to safeguard their farmers, it was decided to cut back production. This meant that they would have to get rid of thousands of cows. Some were slaughtered and others were offered to farmers in the Caribbean, and Central and South America at ridiculous prices.

Many Bajan farmers, including Victor Babb, grabbed the opportunity to increase their herds and their production with these high-producing cheap cows. They were given financing by several banks including Barbados National Bank (BNB).

Unfortunately for Bajan farmers, many of these cows died after succumbing to the heat and/or diseases that they picked up after landing here. Some farmers spent small fortunes with veterinarians in order to save their cows. Others like the landless hand-to-mout farmers soon went out of business.

Victor Babb was still fortunate, he thought. He had land. He could sell off a field here and a field there and pay off the BNB. Thus the Sonnises met their second Babb when Victor decided to sell off some of his land to raise capital. But that was still not enough. Agricultural land has limited value. So Victor Babb thought long and hard. Maybe the fields adjoining John's Plain could be passed for housing. This would allow him some reasonable cash to clear his bank loans and to provide some badly needed working capital to get his dairy farm back into pristine shape.

Unfortunately, Town Planning approval provided for lots that were much too large for a housing development. Unable to finance this development, Victor Babb was once again forced to sell off the fields as large lots. A company called Eastern Developments was the purchaser. In no time flat, the new owners received additional permission for further sub-division. Mr C. O. Williams and Mr. Carl Rayside are two of the owners of Eastern Developments.

In the meantime, Victor Babb continues to struggle. Some people have been highly critical of him as a farmer. I couldn't care less if he is a good farmer or a bad farmer. He cannot be worse than many of the people who ran sugar estates in this country and who milked them dry and ran, or the birds of passage who land here. What matters is how Victor Babb was persistently refused permission and when he was given permission, it was useless and calculated to keep him shackled. A few years later Sandy Lane Hotel had no problem in getting wholesale permission to buy all the agricultural land that made up the rest of Norwoods, Molyneux and Bennetts plantations.

This is a story that can be told over and over again, just change the names. In this case one was named Fielding Babb, a painter who collects and records our patrimony, and the other Victor Babb, a farmer who can't.

The Sonnises, as visitors, collect both. Williams et al collects cows and land which he subdivides and sells. A Babb is not a Babb.

Smelling Hell

I AM a Speightstown man. It was in Speightstown that I learned how to smell. I learned the smell of tamarinds, lying in dead sand being crushed by bare feet and box cart wheels and filling the air with their tanginess. I learned to distinguish the difference in smell between pa-wee mangoes, turpentine mangoes and mango longs.

I learned the smell of the sea, sitting on my Grandmother Beebee's upstairs overhanging verandah when the wind shifted and the trade winds whipped the fishy salt air inland between the Ice House and Plantations Limited.

I learned the smell of pepper and learned how to cool it by eating Aunt Sybil's fishcakes in the sea. I learned the sound of Calypso—*Sly Mongoose* and *Small Island* and *Mary Ann* and *Brown Skin Gal* and *Mama Muh Belly Done Hurt Me* and *Pig Knuckles* and *Rice Tonite*, and *Give Her the Number One*, and the smell of sweat from bodies at the CIVIC Friendly Society Saturday Night doos.

Speightstown is a unique little town. There was a time when jetties abounded at Plantations Limited, at Challenor's, at Wilkinson and Haynes and so on. There were also jetties at Six Men's, just above where Port St. Charles is and Shermans, just below Half Moon Fort.

People used to travel to town (Bridgetown) by schooner in the morning and come back by it in the evening. This was also the means of transporting sugar and general cargo to and from

Speightstown and the North. The *Jolly Roger* and the *Harbour Master* continue the tradition, this time for pleasure between Bridgetown and Speightstown.

Some of the oldest Bajan buildings exist in Speightstown. My love for Speightstown was why I joined the Barbados National Trust Committee that was looking after the restoration of Speightstown. It's well over fifteen years that this plan of restoration for Speightstown has been mooted. But I have never seen an overall plan for Speightstown and its environs.

I have this vision of Speightstown as Barbados' North Coast to distinguish it from the West Coast in terms of a high quality tourism development.

There is not much open beach land left in Speightstown now. Down behind where Sheriff Whitehead used to live and below where the St. Peter Almshouse used to be, is a fisherman's beach peopled by majestic coconut trees, not the poo-poo miniatures, but the stately cousins to the Royal Palms.

To get to this beach, which should be purchased by government and turned into a National Park, you must pass through the old almshouse site. This site is used by the Northern Branch of the Sanitation Department and is not only unsightly with broken-down vehicles (when last I saw it!), but disgustingly smelly from the occasional washings.

The other beach of note, between Six Men's Bay and Shermans, is under threat from erosion and is bordered by the extensive tenantry of Six Men's Plantation.

When the government wanted to develop Heywoods, it moved the road from within yards of the beach to its present location. Other entrepreneurs who developed the eastern side of the road for housing were premature in their efforts to create another Sunset Crest.

Maynard's Plantation on the hill was developed in patches

ranging from government row houses closest to Mile-and-a-Quarter to more upscale villas on the western ridge overlooking Heywoods.

The fact that Heywoods was an Amerindian settlement should not be ignored. There are still areas not yet developed that should be used to recreate this historical feature. It is swampy and should be used imaginatively to enhance the environment and the developments at Almond Beach and Port St. Charles.

And then there is Six Men's Plantation. Nearly 300 acres of former agricultural land that has been out of production for over twenty-five years and bordering what was called a Zone One water area. Sitting on the ridge overlooking the tenantry and Six Men's Bay are eight to ten cannons in expectant promise of battle, the remnants of a once formidable fort, hopefully protecting the owner from the imminent invasion.

On the south side separating Six Men's from Maynards is an extensive gully and a quarry where soft stones and marl were mined. The gully leads down to the sea and with serious engineering could also create an inland marina with housing in the side of the gully walls.

Relocation of the tenantry, giving the present tenants title to their land and relocating the road, would make Six Men's Plantation a perfect complement to the existing tourism plants that are developing to the south. Over 2,000 ft. of beach front would be opened up.

But there is a problem. Six Men's Plantation is owned by a man by the name of C.L. Broome. Mr. Broome was in construction in the early days after Independence and built some houses in Pine Gardens known as Broome's Vacation Homes. He also had some near to the airport. These reasonably priced facilities were used extensively by people from the Islands who had to come to Barbados for USA visas or medical attention or had to overnight before making a connection with LIAT.

Mr. Broome has struggled incessantly to get Six Men's Plantation released for development. He has asked governments of the past to relocate the tenantry and the road to allow him to develop a tourism facility. He had a dream about working with Christians from Canada and the United States to develop a working/training tourism type of facility.

The only difference between Six Men's and Westmoreland is that Westmoreland is probably bigger and was in sugar production more recently. Both shared water restriction covenants. Westmoreland got permission to change from agriculture to recreation (golf course) and tourism. Six Men's has not.

Mr. Broome is a black man.

I fear that Mr. Broome will be persuaded to part with his patrimony for little or nothing. I'll bet the persuader will get the permissions and the considerations of government.

I learned to smell as a boy in Speightstown. Mr. Broome has gone further. He has learned how to smell hell.

The East Coast

ROEBUCK AND Four Hill are two small plantations in St. Peter that are owned by what is called Panama Money. That is, these plantations were purchased from money remitted by Bajans who went to help dig the Panama Canal nearly 100 years ago. Nobody knows who these men were, as time has made a secret of their names.

Up to the 1980s, Roebuck had one of the most interesting small steam-operated sugar mills as well as an old windmill second only to Morgan Lewis.

In the late seventies, a Col. Cave of Nicholas Abbey, with the assistance of the Barbados National Trust, persuaded the Attorney for Roebuck and Four Hill to sell him vital parts from that mill for BDS$1.00 for him to restore his mill at Nicholas Abbey. This restoration was ostensibly for the people of Barbados.

COL. CAVE

Col. Cave owns a short piece of film of the Barbados train traveling along the East Coast of Barbados circa the early 1900s. He had the film restored and about eight copies made. Unfortunately, in spite of a request from the government of Barbados for a videotaped copy for the Barbados Museum, Col. Cave refused.

The area covered by Col. Cave's film is a fascinating one. It is an area wrought with controversy, as can be seen from the environmentalist attack on the Ministry of Health for wanting to site a landfill at Greenland.

When I was a boy, I knew it as the Scotland District, running from Pico Tenerife in the north and ending on College Savannah on the border of St. John and St. Phillip in the south. On the east it was the rugged coastline like a slack rubberband that defined that boundary. On the west, it was the ridge known as Hackleton's Cliff.

Hackleton's Cliff was best known to the country people of St. John and St. Joseph and St. Andrew and to a lesser extent, the people of Boscobel and Cherry Tree Hill in St. Peter who could see it everyday. Cherry Tree Hill encompassed the woods that hid Nicholas Abbey from the public.

The east coast was accessible only to the outing people who travelled by train in the first forty years of this century. I didn't get a chance to travel on it or hear Brumley Brass Band on the way to Cattlewash or Bathsheba or Milady's Passage (Hole?). But I used to see it from Edge Cliff, St. John, from the back of Mrs. Lashley's land where we used to go and chase monkeys.

The East Coast Road was built in the sixties by Errol Barrow who understood the potential of the area. Its opening in 1966 gave all Bajans access to this incredible area. The Scotland District has also been recognized as a special area for development. This has lead to serious arguments and disputes over the last thirty years over what can and cannot be developed.

The expansion of small houses and the increased density of the population, especially in St. Andrew, have been disastrous for the area and have led to the abandonment of several older villages and access roads. The additional roofs and the increase in sizes collected more rain water in small areas and along with water toilets created more and more slippage of the greasy clay soils.

Increased transportation has also contributed to the deterioration of the roads. This is especially true with the wide range of trucks and buses using the roads.

Restoration work was always necessary in the St. Andrew section of the Scotland District. Certainly from the 1950s, such work was undertaken and it was a continuous struggle, especially when cultivation of sugar cane shifted from cane holes to tractor delineated cane rows.

One of the best things to happen to St. Andrew has been the abandonment of sugar cane. The Ministry of Agriculture has been planting fruit trees and other decorative trees in the area. Other parts have been allowed to return to the jungle and this is also a good thing.

In the meantime, sand mining at Walkers continues to be a threat to the area. The East Coast Road and its environs on both sides of the road have been ignored in terms of restoration. There is a need to beautify this area, especially the replanting of the tall, elegant coconut trees and other trees hardy enough to survive the salt wind blast.

With proposed developments at Boscobel, Morgan Lewis, Bath, Codrington College and Apes Hill, the Scotland District is about to face some of its most formidable criticism.

East Coast 2

MR. GILL, the planter, bought Bawdens, Sedge Pond and Rock Hall, according to the folk song, to add to River and the others he owned.

Like the black women in St. Lucy who worked for A.F. Ward, the black women who weeded the cane holes during hard times and headed the bundles of cane up the steep slopes during crop season also kept Mr. Gill's boiler going. Unlike Ward, he never passed on his name to his progeny.

Josh Haynes was also a successful and popular planter and a member of the House of Assembly. He mentored Lloyd Sonny Smith (Boychile), starting him in a trucking business. It is said that Boychile kept a constant check on Mrs. Haynes' whereabouts and kept Josh informed when he was with the plantation help. It is not known what seeds Josh planted, but it is known that the Rocklyn Bus Company sprouted on the bed of Belleplaine.

Oxford, Cambridge, and Bissex are a few of the plantations that Josh Haynes owned. They were also later owned by Mrs. Rock of the Rocklyn Bus Company.

On the eastern side of Cambridge, below Chalky Mount, is an amphitheatre that is like no other in the Caribbean. Once valued cane ground, it now hosts the semi-finals of the Pic-O-de-Crop and the Party Monarch Finals. The site is too valuable and also too fragile to be casually used without long-term planning for amenities, facilities to accommodate the tens of thousands who use it. With careful infrastuctural development, this natural amphitheatre is potentially a big money spinner and visitor attraction.

And what about the general reforestation of the whole of the East Coast Road?

The potential of Chalky Mount itself needs to be examined. There are chemical analyses on the quality and structure of St. Andrew clays. Chalky Mount Village is a valuable tradition that needs to be built on and exploited. Chalky Mount school should have the best teachers and facilities for training the children of Chalky Mount and its environs in ceramic design and production. Claytone is already demonstrating the industrial aspects of these clays at its factory at Greenland, St. Andrew.

It is clear in my mind that to safeguard St. Andrew as an ecosystem, some serious resettlement will have to be considered. I remember the late Froggie Gibbons pointing out to me that he surveyed land in St. Andrew for owners who had no right of way and whose lands had to be eventually abandoned.

Consideration will have to be given to a major resettlement of people from the fragile areas of St. Andrew into the Belleplaine, Haggatts, Lakes, Walkers, Shorey Village plains. In spite of the objections of the two Richards, I support the refilling of the Arawak hole. But I also feel that sand mining at Walkers should be better controlled and termination conditions identified. Those sand dunes are very critical to the area and their total removal will expose the area to serious wind erosion and possible invasion by the sea.

Still going north to Morgan Lewis is the National Trust Windmill. Between the Windmill and Cherry Tree Hill is the up-hill down-hill illusion, an illusion that depends heavily on the terrain around it. Not much is made of this and it is not identified by landmarks.

Before reaching the Windmill, you can pass a goat ranch and

a variety of rams, bulls and cocks on the way to the beach. If it is not rainy, it is possible to cross to one of the most spectacular beaches in Barbados. Completely dominated by natural vegetation, it is privately owned by the late Dr. Bertie Clarke. Potential? Fantastic! At its northern end, this beach goes into what was know as Foster's Funland and Boscobel.

It is said that Boscobel was 'behind God's back'. There was a time when reaching Boscobel was like trying to get to Brazil. But times have changed and with better transportation, this isolation has disappeared.

Boscobel can be best described as rugged and rocky. It definitely was inhospitable to traditional sugar cane agriculture. It was rumoured that you only find wild goats and wild rabbits in and about Boscobel.

The idea that a group of investors are looking at Boscobel for an upmarket type of development has been a long time in coming. St. Andrew needs such a development to stimulate and alter the state of mind of the people of St. Andrew regarding the gold mine that they are sitting on. Many Bajans are benefitting from Port St. Charles, Westmoreland and Sandy Lane. So why shouldn't the people of St. Andrew?

A few years ago when C.O. Williams' nephew, Julian Hunte, developed a hiking tour of the East Coast, through all of these areas, many people thought he was a madman. Julian was never a madman, nor is COW.

East Coast 3

MACKIE SYMMONDS talked as fast as molasses running from a three-gill bottle into a bucket of water when yuh want to make some swank to quench yuh thirst when yuh playing hopping ball cricket in the hot midday sun. It ent dat he talked slow, it was you who was hearing too fast.

MACKIE SYMMONDS

Mackie Symmonds was Algie, Noel and Pat Symmonds' uncle, great uncle to Peter and Donna, father to Dru and grandfather to Kerrie Symmonds.

He established the first black bank in Barbados called the Barbados Co-operative Bank in the late 1930s, and it operated at the corner of Marhill Street and St. Michael's Row.

Mackie Symmonds developed Grazettes Plantation in the 1950s. He was Chairman of the Transport Board and was known to pay wages out of his pocket. When Carrington Village land was being sold out, he lent money to many of the port workers to buy their plots of land.

He was a friend of Errol Barrow, who said at a public meeting that he would not "trust Mackie Symmonds with my son's piggy bank." Needless to say, there was a run on the bank and it collapsed.

But Mackie Symmonds was a pioneer entrepreneur. At a time when Barbados was totally dependent on sugar, Mackie

Symmonds invested in a clay plant to manufacture bricks as an alternative to soft stones for the building of houses and for export. Along with two black Bajan scientists, Arthur Coppin and Nat Carmichael, Mackie Symmonds built a brick factory at Apes Hill Plantation.

Apes Hill Plantation is owned by C.O. Williams, who wants to develop it into an international golf course and tourism facility, although not situated directly on the East Coast. As I said before, I agree with COW.

C.O. Williams is not unlike Mackie Symmonds. Both are developers and both had little interest in sugar cultivation. COW's traumatic experience at Foster Hall Plantation as a boy is one possible explanation for his dislike initially, but certainly he sees more lucrative alternative returns from plantation land. His forays in beef rearing and anthurium lillies, quarrying and land development demonstrate this. But I believe that his experiences in St. Lucia opened his eyes to the true potential of real estate development.

Cutting up and subdividing land is not development.

RONALD TREE

Sandy Lane, when it was developed by Ronald Tree, was aimed at a certain market and for its time was extremely expensive land. There were also strict requirements about the type and design of the house on each lot.

Sunset Crest was seen as an investment for Bajans in a villa concept. Attempts at doing the same at Heywoods were stillborn.

For most Bajans, there developed a perception that Barbados' best land was along the West Coast. As a result, one hears that Barbados is selling its best land to foreigners. Therefore a myth has also developed that the rest of Barbados is not good land.

However, the truth is that a good developer can take nearly any land and make it quality, high-priced land dependent on the features he wants to offer and the market he wants to target.

C.O. Williams' project at Port St. Charles and the ones at Westmoreland and Sandy Lane/Bennetts are similar. There is no reason to believe that Apes Hill and other areas on the East Coast cannot meet these objectives.

As private developers strive to make these projects a reality, especially the golf courses, government must play its part and establish a number of public golf courses for Bajans as well as the not-so-well-off visitors. There is a persistent myth that Barbados has enough golf courses. Approximately 200 persons pass through a golf course daily. Courses attached to luxury homes are mostly reserved for residents and are not available to the general public.

Bermuda has over a dozen golf courses. It is thirty-two square miles big and has a water problem. Each house collects water from its roof and stores it in underground tanks. Bermuda has managed its environment. Barbados can also manage its environment.

Golfing professionals are going to be needed in abundance once more golf courses are developed. We are also going to be required to develop a different type of agricultural specialist. We know a lot about sugar cane, a grass. Can we not learn how to maintain golf course grasses?

Question. What makes Westmoreland more or less valid than any other development?

East Coast 4

CHRISTOPHER CODRINGTON was a bitch. Codrington College in St. John was named after him.

When I was a boy, my father used to take my brother and I to Codrington College for the obligatory Sunday drive. The hallowed quietness of the chapel, no singing, the peopleless grounds, used to subdue our natural rowdiness.

We learned the legend of this supposedly Christian and humanitarian man who bequeathed his wealth to the Anglican Church in England through the Society for the

CHRISTOPHER CODRINGTON

Propagation of the Gospel (SPG). After Independence in 1966, the SPG handed over the seven hundred plus acres and the college to the Codrington Trust.

Apparently, Mr. Codrington, a bachelor, had no children. Planters had difficulty acknowledging their progeny, especially those from African women. Mr. Codrington owned hundreds of slaves, and to prevent them from running away, he branded them (men, women and children) with CC on their chests like how American cowboys branded cattle.

Christopher Codrington was a bitch.

Actually, there were three Christopher Codringtons—father, son and holy grandson—so take your pick.

Most Bajans are unaware that Codrington College owns as much land as it does or that most of the houses at Consett Bay occupy lands leased from the Codrington Trust or that the Lodge School is also a long-term occupant.

St. John is unique in Barbados' social history. The movers and shakers of the parish have traditionally kept the poor (both black and white) of the parish in bondage. And although the Codrington Trust (and the SPG before that) is a major landholder in the parish, its presence has never been felt as a progressive institution in the parish.

The idea that the Codrington Trust is now willing to release about 400 acres for a major real estate development can and will trigger consequential developments that will benefit the people of St. John, St. Phillip, St. George and St. Joseph.

How much has the Codrington Estate given back to the people of Barbados? I argued with Errol Barrow and Cammie Tudor that Codrington College should have been used as the site for the Barbados campus of the University of the West Indies. They didn't buy it.

Now we have the option of what essentially will be the development of a golf course with its adjunct and concomitant upmarket housing. A golf course is expensive to develop and it is usually paid for by the housing development on and about the greens.

This development will offer both short-term and long-term employment to the people in the surrounding areas. Most such developments end up as resort areas and therefore there is a continuous need to service such a development.

There are three fishing villages along the East Coast which are important: Tent Bay in St. Joseph, at the south end of Bathsheba;

Consett Bay in St. John; and Skeete's Bay in St. Phillip. Is it too farfetched to believe that there are tourists who would want to join our traditional fishermen for a day of fishing?

Or is it beyond belief to imagine that the people of St. Margaret's and Martin's Bay can organize a Friday Night Fish Fry at Martin's Bay?

There is also talk that there are Taiwanese investors interested in Bath Plantation. This is where I draw a line. From Walkers to Bath must be kept for Bajans to develop a more indigenous resort area that is affordable to them and reflects more our distinct cultural heritage. This includes Bathsheba and Cattlewash.

Nothing in these articles must be construed as suggesting that these developments must not be carefully and precisely managed. All the specific regulations for sewage and waste disposal, water, roads, use of pesticides, etc., ecological protection, and terracing must be put in place. We must not assume that such developments cannot do this. Once we know what we have and want to protect it and pass it on to our progeny, then we can insist on the standards that are necessary to guarantee this.

For too long we have allowed tourism facilities to be developed ad hoc. To date we have not identified Barbados' carrying capacity for tourism. We have also not zoned our beach land, decided on the market mix, nor have we decided how to guarantee that people are able to reach us.

The East Coast is one of our most precious areas. It has benefitted from the abandonment of sugar cultivation in that many areas have become reforested. It has been a combination of some planning, but mostly it has been a result of neglect due to a perception that it no longer has an economic value.

Port St. Charles, Westmoreland and Sandy Lane have indicated that economic value can be created. And in spite of all that I have written, we as a people must decide how we are to benefit from all of these developments.

The Future Is Now, Let Us Plan

IN WRITING about the East Coast over the last few weeks, I am cognizant of the enormous pressures to allow development in the area and of the concomitant objections to any such development.

Some time ago government declared that the East Coast, from St. Lucy to St. Phillip, was to be a park. What that means is yet to be defined, but it was generally accepted that the area would be subject to special regulations and considerations.

St. Andrew, St. Joseph and St. John have given up on sugar cane agriculture. Farmers in these parishes struggle incessantly with many alternative forms of agriculture: dairy farming (both cow and goat), beef rearing, black belly sheep loving, pig farming, fruit and vegetable farming, and so forth. For most, if not 90 percent of the farmers, agriculture is a part-time activity.

Prime Minister Owen Arthur and former Central Bank Guru Dr. DeLisle Worrell have both predicted an end to agrarian activity in Barbados in the next decade, although Dr.

DELISLE WORRELL

Worrell focused on the future of commercial agriculture.

Errol Barrow once suggested that he would not like to see a single cane blade on the Barbados horizon. C.O. Williams has made the same suggestion. Barrow had the political power and did very little to implement his idea.

Perhaps the time had not come. Williams has the economic power and has set about dismantling the sugar industry on most of the plantations he owns.

What are the likely alternatives?

Both the BLP and DLP governments as well as numerous technocrats and private sector chiefs have recognized the need to alter Barbados' dependency on the sugar industry, and bit by bit have consciously, accidentally or passively created alternatives.

Barbados' future must therefore be centred around the supply of services to the rest of the world. Whether or not these services are in tourism, finance or informatics!

Bajans must alter their perception of the world and become more proactive in getting what they want for our people. We, and that means all of us, must determine as soon as possible what we want from the world and set about organizing how we are going to achieve it.

We must cease the practice of believing we have to make a living off of each other when there is a big world out there off which to make a living. When I write metaphorically about the egrets, I want us to be like egrets living symbiotically with the rest of the world. Cut and contrive as a strategy.

The people of and on the East Coast must not be passive observers to the development process on the East Coast. In the same way that they reacted to the Greenland landfill, they must also become active participants in determining their future and make inputs in the plans for the area.

The East Coast is going to have to accommodate all the things that make up the rest of Barbados: parks, landfills, mining, agriculture, resorts, settlements, recreation and sporting facilities including golf courses, and all the other activities that Bajans want.

All of these can be achieved with a difference. For example, why not value all the resources in the area, set up a development company to take over all of these assets, and issue shares to all of the owners and their heirs. Alternatively, these lands could be leased for fifty years with rights for renewal for another fifty years. This would guarantee that future generations would still be able to share in the ownership and wealth of the country.

By doing this, the central development company would be able to control the quality and quantity of the development on the East Coast to make it compatible with national objectives.

Is it possible to do these things?

Yes. When government had a functioning Community Development Department, it was able to assist with the development of the Sewage Plant at Emmerton Lane by holding extensive meetings with residents in the area. The end result was that residents volunteered to move and were smoothly relocated to Clapham.

When there was a problem with beach vendors, the National Cultural Foundation, which had responsibility for Community Development (and rightly so) assisted in establishing the Beach Vendors' Association and the Water Sports Association by holding meetings with the people involved.

The future is now, let us plan.

Duppies, Spirits and Ancestors

Duppies, Spirits and Ancestors

"I doan believe in duppies, but I frighten fuh dem."

A respectable Bajan lady

GRANNIE BEBE house in Speightstown is right pon de road. Before the Naval Base trucks lick it off, there was an upstairs gallery that we used to use to watch the schooners set sail for town pon a morning and return pon a evening.

The dust from the road layered the furniture in the front house like a fresh coat of paint. The white-head bush bleached floors were always covered with sand

BEBE COLLINS

trekked in on our feet from the beach behind Plantations Limited.

Grannie Bebe was always dusting and sweeping to get rid of the dust and sand. During the day, she would sweep everything from the house through the backdoor into the yard. But in the evening she would always sweep the dust and sand into a corner and then remove it in the morning.

It never occurred to me that there was a difference. I never asked her why she did it. She died and I never had the opportunity to ask. But many years later I heard people saying that you don't sweep out the house at night because you will bring bad luck to the house.

In trying to understand our culture, I discovered that this idea of not sweeping out a house at night belongs to a long African tradition. Apparently, in African tradition, it is expected that at night all the spirits of the ancestors enter the house at sunset. Some of these spirits are good and some are evil. If you sweep out the house at night, you are liable to sweep out the good spirits and leave the bad ones. When that happens, bad luck will befall the house.

Because of the Eurocentric nature of our educational system, many of these beliefs are lost or misunderstood. Like the lady I quoted above, many people don't believe in spirits (duppies), but they are afraid of them. And therein lies the essence of our African being.

Some years ago when I was a member of the board of the Barbados Museum, I discovered some papers written by an American Professor by the name of Jerry Handler. Prof. Handler had with a number of students discovered a slave burial ground at Newton Plantation in Christ Church.

The story of this burial ground was unfolded in a series of papers written by Handler and his associates. I was also at the time head of the National Cultural Foundation. I took the decision to use Newton Plantation for the official opening of the Crop Over Festival.

That opening was one with a difference. We decided to share the information that Handler and his associates discovered about the life of the Africans in slavery with the general public.

And so we selected students from the Community College to act as guides and explain to patrons at the opening what exactly was discovered by this group of archaeologists and anthropologists. The students were trained by our Research

Officer historian Trevor Marshall. We also prepared visuals with the assistance of the Barbados Museum.

The burial ground is situated on the north side of the Newton Plantation yard on a field of rab land. Realizing that this was prime land for development, I called Senator Ward who was either the owner or attorney for the land and asked him if he would donate it to the Barbados Museum. He readily agreed and eventually it was handed over to the Barbados Museum.

I must thank Senator Ward, a white Bajan, for his appreciation for the importance of this burial ground to the people of Barbados and his generous donation that will lead to greater understanding of our heritage. The Barbados Museum has recently undertaken a series of new studies on the burial ground and I trust that further information will be forthcoming from these studies.

However, as we celebrate Emancipation each year, we must remind ourselves of the fact that Africans considered it was better to die in the Middle Passage or wherever they were, to allow their spirits to return home to Africa.

I think it is therefore incumbent on us to establish a symbolic closure for our ancestors by returning one of these remains back to the continent of Africa. Of course this effort must be attended by traditional rituals. Therefore we must invite those in Africa to come here to appease the spirits and take the body for a ritual reburial in the homeland.

The depth of our being is yet to be unfolded.

A Story: Swain and the Sturges Duppy

Characters:

Corporal Lashley - narrator, policeman, driver to Sir Allan Collymore.
Young Swain - young white man, plantation manager's son, popular in Sturges Village.
Black Boy - a.k.a. monkey, duppy.
Duke - white Antiguan, Commissioner of Police.
Sir Allan Collymore -white Chief Justice of Barbados
Grantley Adams - black lawyer, political/trade union leader, parliamentarian.
E. Keith Walcott - white lawyer, Attorney-General, parliamentarian.
Erskine Ward - lawyer, son of a white planter and a black woman.
Jury - twelve black men.

Plot:

In Sturges Village, St. Thomas, a little Black Boy carefreely chases butterflies in a field of young cane. And sweet potato slips that wrap the rim of cane-holes to form vases for the fledgling blades grab at he foot in mock sport. Without warning. Bahdai! And a riffle of lead pellets, like rockstones from a bundle of guttaperks, like the one still in he back pocket, rip off Black Boy face from he ear to he cheekbone and leave he jawbone ajar.

Dead.

Young Swain says he thought Black Boy was a monkey—a four-leg Buh Monkey—tiefing potatoes. Young Swain is arrested. Charged, but never jailed. He just lives in the police station. And Sturges people vex vex.

E. K. Walcott, as Attorney-General, rules Barbados as has all Attorneys-General have done since Conrad Reeves in the 1870s. He is the last such leader as constitutional changes shift power to a Premier. He resigns as AG rather than prosecute Young  Swain for murder. Walcott is a political realist. Cocky and feisty like a bantam cock in three piece dark-blue serge suits, he knows in his heart that he cannot use his prodigious prosecuting skills against Young Swain. If he does, Swain would hang. Instead, he resigns.

And as much as he detests his political

E.K. WALCOTT rival Grantley Herbert Adams, he recommends that Young Swain hire this black trade union and political leader to defend him before a jury of twelve black men.

Grantley Herbert Adams, Barbados Scholar, lawyer, politician, trade unionist, black leader, defender of the faith, agrees to defend Young Swain for killing little Black Boy, whom he thought was a monkey. Adams is to be paid in guineas. He fuhmember when James A. Tudor used to have to send Cammie personally with the free groceries to he house at Tyrol Cot. He fuhmember the summonses with the four corners burn off and nuff nuff burn holes and the slime from the crappeau mout and de shillings, never pounds or guineas.

Grantley Herbert Adams is Young Swain's salvation. It is not going to be an easy task against the young, brilliant, acerbic Erskine Ward, a man who he shares whore-house rooms with.

Erskine Ward is a lawyer. One brother is a lawyer too and another is a doctor. He is the son and grandson of white Bajan planters. His mother is a black woman. His black cousins ramble in the sour-grass fields round plantation land and live in tenantries like Sturges Village. He fuhmember running thru cane ground tripping pun lying canes and falling in muddy cane holes.

As a matter of fact he fuhmember how he grandfather mek he and he brothers and sister eat in de kitchen and not wid he white cousins in the dining room of the great house. And he fuhmember the ride in de buggy back to town and how vex he father did and how he never ever went back to that great house.

Commissioner Duke is a white Antiguan. He is different from Bajan whites. He is very friendly with all de black lawyers and doctors and plays tennis with them at Summerhayes Club in Belleville. Bajan whites doan like this and clamour for the Colonial Office to remove him. So he won't listen to the pleadings and warnings from the planters and merchants.

Sir Allan Collymore doan talk to blacks, he talk bout blacks, especially while in the back seat of he car. He doan like the political changes in Barbados. He doan like trade unions. He also doan like monkeys and doan know nutten bout duppies and crappeaus.

Corporal Lashley is a policeman and Sir Allan's driver. He telling dis story.

The Trial:

Young Swain is convicted and given only 18 months. He serves a year. On release he leaves Barbados for parts unknown.

Black Boy duppy still chasing butterflies.

A Wake for Brother Brown

JAMAICA IS blessed with mountains of unbelievable contours. Womanly. Mountains crested with plumes of bamboos. Mountains plaited with slender cedars and giant guangoes. Mountains cornrowed with midget coffee trees. Mountains afroed by plump mangoes and dreadlocked ackees!

And in between, bottomless valleys of foliage-cups catching clouds of mists and myriad butterflies.

Hidden away from distant eyes are homes and villages and people galore. Yet, like the proverbial jungle drums, there are sounds singing through the leaves, threading like vines the several hillsides.

It's one of the things I am yet to get accustomed to—to not be able to see the houses or the people in the hills. You pass them and you see them. You look back and they have disappeared. No roads. No houses. No people. Just trees. But you can hear the sounds.

The hills of Northern Clarendon can never be considered the Blue Mountains of Upper St. Andrew. But one thing about them is that they are all alive with the sound of music. When I was a boy living in Tudor Bridge, Barbados, you could walk from Water Hall Land to Grazettes Corner and hear everything that was on Radio Distribution (the name before Rediffusion Services bought it out). It was like an echo. Everybody used to have the speaker in the front house in the corner by the window so that when they looking out, they could hear the request program or the soap opera pon a evening. It was like walking along the aisles of a supermarket with its wall-to-wall sound.

Not so in Jamaica. The sounds cascade through the hills, coming from there or from over there or from down in the valley or cross pon that next hill. It is all over the place. Different sounds. The sounds of reggae, of dancehall, of rock steady, of ska. The sounds of Jamaica.

That is what we heard as we climbed into the hills of Northern Clarendon to attend Brother Brown's set-up. Some call it a singing, but it was a wake. The wake was in its sixth day and still had three to go.

It was like a political meeting. Cars were parked up to two miles from the house in all directions on every road and every track, in every yard and at every gate. There were buses, trucks, pickups, cars, and motorcycles.

People came from all over Jamaica. They came from Kingston, May Pen, Santa Cruz, Port Antonio. They were family, friends and acquaintances. They were lawyers, doctors, judges, politicians (local and national) from all parties, farmers, neighbours, and plain old folks.

Brother Brown's house was a low, sprawling edifice set about twenty feet from the road. On the left front of the house was a massive ackee tree. On the other side was a long garage running the length of the house and capable of holding at least three trucks and a car. In fact, it only held an old nineteen sixty-ish American pickup.

The rest of the yard was covered by a huge tarpaulin under which about fifteen women were preparing food in huge pots: curry goat, fried chicken, rice and peas, roast breadfruit, and, of course, mannish-water in abundance.

In front the house, across the road, on an empty lot which was recently debushed, were two bars under tarpaulins propped up by six-inch-thick bamboo poles. White rum (no red rum for Jamaicans) and Ting and Red Stripe and soft drinks were available to all.

And all the while the sound system kicking with familiar songs which from time to time everyone started singing. And so it went until four or five in the morning. This is how it was for the last week and still two days to go before the funeral.

At the funeral, which took place at the small 150-seat village church, hundreds came. They were scattered all over the road. The village shops did great business for the evening.

Then I realized that Brother Brown was to be buried in front of his house under the massive ackee tree. This is not so unusual, as throughout Jamaica you will see headstones and white-washed tombs on most of the country land. It is not just a matter of your navel string being buried there, but also your remains.

But who was this Brother Brown who attracted so many people to his wake over the last week and to his funeral that Saturday evening? Brother Brown was what you can describe as a village chief. He had a pickup in which he transported people's goods and belongings from Kingston, from May Pen or even from the Norman Manley Airport.

In this area where public transport is poor or non-existent, Brother Brown provided transport for all. He took the farmers' produce to the market. He took the sick to the doctor or hospital. He gave lifts to people going into town or coming home at night.

And he was a political canvasser. He intervened on behalf of people to their representative regardless of party. He identified people for jobs. He took care of the old and the young. Brother Brown was an old-time leader who took his role seriously, and the people knew.

As I was leaving, I took a look at his tombstone; it was in the shape of his pickup truck, trimmed in a bright sky blue. Farewell

Brother Brown.

New legislation has been introduced to limit the plethora and loudness of sound systems of Jamaica.

Roots Revisited

IN THE mid-60s, just after Barbados got its Independence, I spent most of my time traveling to every nook and cranny of Barbados to get first-hand knowledge of the whole island and talking to people to find out about times past.

One of the most interesting moments was interviewing an old woman somewhere around Middleton in St. George. I was looking for people to talk to about bush medicine and was directed to her. Her house was about twenty feet from the cart road, perched on what seemed to be a ledge above a gully.

The house was surrounded by overgrown bush. Actually, there were gardens of different bushes she cultivated and used to sell in front of the CIVIC at the corner of Swan and High Streets in Bridgetown. The roof was either trash or grass, which surprised me. The paths around the house were hard dirt. No weeds. The house faced the side, not the road, and that was where the entrance was. There were no steps to enter the house, since the floor was also dirt.

The old woman wore her hair tied with a white cloth covered by a broad-brimmed Panama straw hat. You could only see a few plaits of hair protruding below the headtie. Her clothes were not colourful, but consisted of various layers topped with a large three-pocket apron. Her face was pleasant and friendly, and she had a habit of laughing and covering her face with the crook of her right arm when she did.

We sat in the door-mout of the house; she on a bench and I on a rock, she shelling pigeon peas in her lap and I posing questions about this and that. I got a lesson about bushes and teas to treat colds, fevers, bad feels, rheumatism, neuralgia, bellyhurt, lining colds, morning sickness, miscarriages, toothaches, lice, chiggers, sores, cuts, stump-toes, nail-jooks. Name it, she had a remedy for any and everything.

Then she tell me bout the church. The Anglican Church. She tell me how she didn't like the church cause the white people didn't like them to come in there pon a Sunday. She said that she preferred the Church Army that used to march through the village on Wednesday nights singing Sankeys and beating tambourines. She liked church services that had a beat.

When I asked her about the riots (the 1937 Riots) and what she remembered, she said she only knew what her mother told her. How the white people wanted to make them slaves again and how the people had to riot and get on bad to stop them. She said her mother say that it was cat piss and pepper all over Buhbadus.

JOHN POPE HENNESEY

That the Queen had set them free and now the planters wanted to take way their freedom.

What the hell was she talking bout? 1937? No, the 1875 Federation Riots, when the Governor John Pope Hennessy wanted to make Barbados a Crown Colony to break the power of the planters.

I was surprised at this memory link. It was the first time I was hearing a report from the nineteenth century other than by an academic historian.

Over the Christmas holidays, I sat with my sons and had a look at Alex Haley's *Roots* for the first time in almost twenty

ALEX HALEY

years. *Roots* is a story born of a memory passed down seven generations to Alex Haley about an African ancestor called Kunta Kinte who refused to forsake his memory of his home in Africa, his family or his freedom.

A monumental work that took twelve years to research, *Roots* portrayed for the first time on the mass media, the continuum between black people in Africa and black people in the Americas. It showed vividly the conditions that Africans had to endure on the slave ships in the Middle Passage, the humiliation at the hands of white slavers in the Americas, and the cruelty suffered at the hands of ignorant overseers.

Evident too is the contradiction between the law and the reality of day-to-day existence. African Americans were treated as animals and defined by the law as such. Yet Backra men (men of authority who happen to be white) found it necessary to rape the black woman time and time

MEN IN SLAVERY

again. As a result of this, many of us have little problem tracing our lineage—our roots—to our European ancestors.

Unfortunately, tracing our roots to Africa through family becomes a very tenuous exercise unless we are descended from some of the Africans who migrated to the Caribbean (for example, Trinidad and Tobago) during the latter half of the nineteenth century.

MASS LYNCHING

American and European television have portrayed generations of European families in epic stories, whether as documentary or as fiction, each calculated to reinforce a sense of being, a sense of tradition. When Alex Haley wrote *Roots*, he recognized that for African peoples, our links to our origins cannot only be measured in the broad cultural continuities and transmissions, such as an understanding of bush medicine or tropical agriculture or religiosity, but in the stories about the trials and tribulations of individuals who have been able to conquer the circumstances of their existence.

Hollywood has a habit of glamorizing situations for the screen. In *Roots*, housing and clothing seem out of proportion to the conditions of the time. I have to say this when I recall the condition of the old lady's house in St. George in the mid 1960s, or the conditions of many of the share-croppers in the Southern United States during the Civil Rights Movement of the 1960s, much of it reported on the news of the day.

African peoples of the New World, that is, the Americas, survived slavery. How and why we did has still not been shown to us. Yet a week doesn't pass without all of us getting reminders on some television show about the horrors of the holocaust against the Jews by the Germans during World War II. The lesson of course is that the holocaust must never happen again to Jews.

In *Roots*, Kunta Kinte made it clear too that although he was physically enslaved and that one of his feet was severed at the instep to prevent him from escaping, his mind was not enslaved. He sought freedom to be, freedom to raise his family, freedom to be free. His resistance to enslavement was an ongoing battle.

We must never lose sight of this.

Gathering of the Generations, Part I

"Ever seen
a man
travel more
seen more
lands
than this poor
land-
less, harbour-
less spade?"

Edward Kamau Brathwaite, Rights of Passage

LOUIS TULL and I were among the first Bajan Students to attend the University of Manitoba in Winnipeg, Canada, in the late fifties. During some of the summers we worked on the trains as porters. He tells the story of travelling around 1961 to The Pas, a desolate mining town about 400 miles north of Winnipeg.

As he stepped off the train to prepare for the passengers departure, he encountered an elderly (probably in his seventies) black man who greeted him. There was instant recognition. His accent. A Bajan in this forlorn unknown town halfway to the Hudson Bay and the legendary RCMP outposts. It turned out that he was a former porter who settled in The Pas after his retirement.

In 1985-6, I visited Vancouver with a delegation from the Board of Tourism, the NCF and the Government Information Service to plan Barbados' participation in the Canadian Exposition in

Vancouver. While there, we discovered a restaurant called 'Joe Fortes' named after a legendary figure who was part of the early settlement of Vancouver in the late nineteenth/early twentieth century.

We soon discovered that Joe Fortes was a Bajan who worked his way up the Pacific coast from Panama, established himself as the 'Original Beach Bum', living on the beach and, according to his obituary, teaching almost everybody in Vancouver to swim.

By the way, he is the spitting image of George Forte who used to be at Sandy Lane for so many years. I surmise that Joe Fortes was probably part of that large number of Bajans who went to Panama to help build the Panama Canal and changed his name by adding an 's' to make it sound more Spanish. This was something many Bajans did in Panama to avoid discrimination.

During CARIFESTA in Havana, Cuba, in 1979, I had the privilege of meeting a young lady who was twenty-something and who was a Senator in Panama. She had one plea. She was a descendent of Bajans and she wanted Barbados to help in re-establishing relations with Bajans in Panama. She knew and could perform the Maypole Dance, she knew the old folk songs and the rhythms of the Tuk Band. It is a good idea because there will be a lot of good material that is locked in time that we can access.

Many Bajans had altered their names to Spanish-sounding names in order to remain and to survive in Panama. I have no doubt that the New York-based Panamanian Reuben Blades (pronounced Blah-days), presidential candidate, actor, singer, intellectual, is of Bajan stock. (Tony Best can check that out!)

Ambassador Val McComie used to tell

REUBEN BLADES

171

of a Bajan taxi driver that he encountered on the Brazilian/ Venezuela border.

These stories are similar to many that any West Indian can tell. Each country has numerous stories of how its citizens have found themselves scattered like seeds on the wind to the far-flung corners of the world. And today we are still migrating and still moving.

But what about inviting them back for a visit? All of them, not just one generation, but all of the generations.

Think of the economic power that all of these West Indians would have. Consider the fact that they there are more West Indians outside of the West Indies than in the West Indies. What about bringing them all back in the year 2000?

Think of it, a *Gathering of the Generations* in the Caribbean…

Hotels and airlines could offer special fares to persons who can demonstrate their West Indian origins. With the Montego Bay hub, one can spend part of the vacation in different countries. All the Festivals in the region could organize to meet the demands of our cousins and their families who will come throughout the year to benefit from the special offers. Seminars and conferences can be organized in all aspects of our culture.

Think of the merchandising and souvenirs that can be developed to cater to this market. The tours, the car rentals, the events, the exhibitions. I cannot imagine a limit to the entrepreneurship that would develop to meet the needs of the Generations.

The marketing for this project should start in 1998 using every West Indian connection including the internet.

What is required? National committees and a single Regional committee made up from and involving the Caribbean Tourism Organisation, the Caribbean Hotel Association, the National Tourism Organisations and the numerous sporting associations.

Even though the *Gathering of the Generations* is slated for the year 2000, I am suggesting that this is only the beginning of what can be done.

For example, we should start preparing a database of all of these West Indians, their addresses, their skills so that we can develop an international lobby group especially in the USA and UK. Don't underestimate the power of a cohesive grouping of West Indians wherever they are.

We have seen their influence. Wherever we find carnivals being celebrated, we know that there is a substantial population of West Indians in that community. It is one of the reasons we should start a massive support for these diaspora festivals.

The proposed seminars and conferences are to orient the *Generations* about some of the roles that they can play in their home towns. We can also expose them to potential investment in their home countries. Most of all, we can arm them with knowledge of themselves to strengthen their bonds with the Caribbean. We should also recognize their achievements and in so doing we would have created a new and major market.

Maybe nobody has travelled as much or as diversely as we have. Let us now take advantage of these resources and mine them for our development.

Gathering the Generations, Part 2

THERE IS no place in the world like the Caribbean. No place. There are no people like Caribbean people. Whether we are Amerindian, European, African or Indian, we have been captured, enslaved or indentured. Cargo-ed, chattel-ed and civilized (Europeanized). Defiled, maligned and defined.

Like flotsam on the tides of time, we took to the seas seeking and searching for the promised land. Like winged seeds, we rode the winds along the trade routes to London, Paris, Amsterdam, New York, and Montreal seeking a living—life away from the long Tamarind season on the plantations of the Caribbean.

We migrated in search of self, for something better. And yet, we never lost the memory of home. The West Indies, the Caribbean. There was a time, a long long time ago when that home was Africa, Europe or India. After that, it was the Caribbean. The last memory.

As the century closes, there are generations in England, Holland, France, Canada and the USA whose connections with the Caribbean are fading. Yet, there are those who are keeping the memories alive with carnivals and other activities.

The Caribbean must see these cousins as Caribbean People and establish a means to hold them to our bosoms first as family and secondly as a cultural force for social, political and economic action.

Let me cite two examples of how this force can work.

The Cuban community in Miami has the power to lobby the US Congress to bring about the *Helms-Burton Act*. The second was an incident that took place in Brooklyn preceding the Labour Day Carnival. A container of Banks Beer scheduled for distribution to shops and booths for the Monday Bank Holiday was held by customs on Friday evening. Customs said it would not be released until the Tuesday after Labour Day. Senator Joe Kennedy of New York had it released on Saturday.

Labour Day Carnival attracted the mayor of New York and other officials, sponsorship by the *Daily News*, radio coverage on several radio stations and over 3 million spectators on the road. Caribana in Toronto attracts over a million. Notting Hill in the UK even more.

This weekend's meeting between the CARICOM heads of government and President Clinton has been emphasizing the need for the region to act as a block or as a singular Caribbean State.

Whenever a society is threatened by an external force, it closes ranks under a common ideal. Finally, we are hearing talk about a Caribbean State. I agree with this, but it is also important that we establish within our Caribbean communities strong lobbying groups to assist in the defense of our own culture(s).

Caribbean governments must begin to see the necessity in supporting overseas festivals as vehicles for Caribbean identity and marketing of the Caribbean.

Gathering the Generations is meant to achieve this.

We must begin to see that the market for Caribbean products and services is also Caribbean people themselves wherever they are settled. Caribbean People are serviced by Koreans in Brooklyn, New York (and in several other cities), who supply Caribbean foods which, no doubt, probably come from other than Caribbean sources.

Our tourism industry is delicately dependent on continuous good news of the Caribbean. Caribbean People have no such delusions. Coming from the region, they have independent contacts to investigate the slurs and arrows hurled by an ignorant and prejudiced American Press.

Gathering the Generations, then, can bring about an awareness of Caribbean People in the metropoles. Their involvement as special visitors will counterbalance the dependency on good rumour. *Gathering the Generations* will bring in an additional US$10 billion to the region in the year 2000.

The first thing that is required is a calender of events for the year 2000—festivals, concerts, exhibitions, sporting events, conferences, expositions, major lectures, and so forth. This calender should list dates, times and locations for all activities. It should be published in magazine format as well as electronically on the internet in English, French and Spanish. The deadline for this publication should be the middle of 1998. Updates will follow.

To publish such a calender will obviously require the planning of such events from now. Many of which are now fairly well set. For example, the Carnivals, Crop-Over, the Jazz Festivals, Pan Festivals, and the myriad music festivals across the Caribbean.

Sports festivals are a must. Test Cricket, Red Stripe Cup and the Sandals one-day, Under 19 and Under 15, Gary Sobers Youth Tournament and any other one-day specials that can be organized. Athletic meets featuring the cream of West Indian athletes, CARIFTA Games, PanAm Games, Regional Meets as well as National Meets like the Boys' and Girls' Champs in Jamaica and the Louis Lynch Games in Barbados. CONCACAF football competitions.

These are only some of the ideas vis-à-vis *Gathering the Generations*. But who should take the initiative in establishing the concept? The Tourist Board? The Ministry of Tourism? The Hotel Association? The Chamber of Commerce? The Ministry of Trade? The Ministry of Education and Culture? The Caribbean Tourism Organisation? The Caribbean Development Bank? The Prime Minister?

When I see the litany of complaints coming out of the CARICOM/USA summit, *Gathering the Generations* from the USA, Canada, UK and Europe is a priority.

Let us kill the fatted calves and welcome home the prodigals.

ELOMBE MOTTLEY

Black Night: Footsteps in Front

Black Night: Footsteps in Front

KEITH PAYNE'S Fishnet Bar and Restaurant was in Milk Market, that vague area between where Baxter's Road ends and Tudor Street begins and ends, and Broad Street, obliquely opposite James Street. It was a one-door establishment reminiscent of a Harlem storefront, but had its origins in days long gone when it was a shop for the owners who lived upstairs.

The door was almost as wide as the room itself and swallowed people at lunchtime like a hungry shark. Not that it was large; it seated maybe thirty persons at most at the bar and the six or seven small tables that were scattered around the room. It was an eight to four place. Actually, Keith was one of the few young men who parlayed an inheritance into a business of his own. The Fishnet assured his independence.

So when Keith offered us the use of the Fishnet, we readily accepted.

Barbados had achieved political Independence a few years before, but little was done to refocus the country on the parameters of what this meant. Coincidentally, this Independence came at a time when there was a worldwide awakening by the African Diaspora. Black people were redefining and renaming themselves, asserting their humanity, and demanding power commensurate with their citizenship. But none of these processes were incorporated into policy by the government of Barbados at Independence. Barbados sought these things for itself as a country in the outside world, but not for its citizens internally.

In spite of the fact that we had produced writers of the calibre of George Lamming, Edward Kamau Brathwaite, and Frank Collymore among others, very little was known of them by the population at large. And to our consternation, we found that theatre was dominated by expatriates with productions that did not reflect us at this new and bristling period.

The founding of the Barbados National Theatre Workshop attempted to meet this need. The African-American writer, Lorraine Hansberry's *A Raisin in the Sun* came closest to this but the paucity of original Barbadian works put paid to any serious pursuit of this ideal. We needed writers.

Keith Payne's invitation gave us an opportunity to tackle the paucity of our situation.

With enthusiasm we established *Black Night*, a platform for developing and exposing budding writers, performers and thinkers that met every Sunday night at the Fishnet.

There were writers like Timmy Callender, Kofi Akobi (Bodger Gittens), Tony Thompson, Milton McCollin, Stanley Mayers, Ray Rahaman, Adam Wade, Boo Rudder, Robert Lee and Alwyn Bully; drummers like el Verno del Congo (Verne Best), Freddie Best, street troubadours like Shilling, Lindy Bradshaw and Bones, and recording/sound engineer Livy Jordan. There were others, some from Trinidad and Tobago, Jamaica, Guyana, St. Lucia and elsewhere.

The crowd sat on the floor on old newspapers, lying in each other's lap. It overflowed on to the sidewalk, into the middle of the road. New poems, new short stories, chapters from unfinished novels, explorations into rhythm poetry, and most of all the soul-stirring and inspirational works of Kamau in Nation Language. And the revelations of Shilling the street-wise philosopher, the ever silent Lindy Bradshaw who spoke through his inimitable guitar stylings.

Black Night was an outpouring of creative energy. Out of *Black Night* came Yoruba Yard.

Writers Workshop paralleled *Black Night*: Robert Morris, Tony Hinkson, Margaret Gill, Ben Craig, Arnold Ward, Earl Warner, Winston Farrell, Victor Clifford, Mark Alleyne, and Martin Ramsay: all of us seeking to define ourselves, to name ourselves, to define our identities.

What has happened to all of this writing?

A decade and a half ago, the National Cultural Foundation had a play-writing competition. Many of the entries were more suited for movie or television scripts than for the stage. But there was a strong indication that people were willing to try. Unfortunately that competition was abandoned.

John Gilmore, Adisa and the Gilkes Brothers followed *Black Night* with their explorations at the Pink Star in Baxters Road in the eighties. NIFCA continues to be an annual platform for many, particularly the youth. But where has all of this work gone?

The fine artists and the sculptors have their exhibitions. The calypsonians, the Euro-classicists, the jazz musicians, the gospel fraternity have their concerts? Where are the publications by and for the literary artists? Where is BIM and BANJA?

Glenville Lovell, in his novel *Fire in The Canes*, reminds us: "Before you walk in your own footsteps, you ought to know who footsteps in front you." Let us let the youth see and hear the footsteps in front of them. Publish, publish, publish!

Wuhlay Wuhloss, Bajan to Dead?

"The revolution (in communication) is the development of a new youth language and a commitment to destruction of the existing standards of oral and written communication.... It is not even Bajanese because most of it is taken from the Caribbean Society of Jamaica, and the remainder comes from the 'Rap' culture of the urban ghettoes of North America particularly New York."

Trevor G. Marshall, 'Standard English for Schools',
Action, December 31, 1999

WHEN I used to teach at the Modern High School, I had a major problem communicating with children in a class in Commerce. The text book was an English (country) text book with references to business in the UK. After much frustration in trying to explain the concepts of commerce I decided to start with what the children knew.

I then asked the children to explain to me what dem mother or grandmother used to do when dem had a old fowl or old duck to cook. In nuh time, all hands went up: she does use green pawpaw leaves or she does cut up green pawpaw. It was easy to lead them from that to commerce. During the whole exercise I used Bajan in its purist form.

Let me mek it clear from up front. I believe that we should learn and be taught the English language. Let me also mek it clear that speaking English will always be an advantage in a world where English is the language of power and the powerful. It cannot be an advantage in China unless yuh writing manuals on how to use computers and other electronic equipment that

English-speaking people going to use.

But English is a funny ting. The English, that is, people born in England, the Irish, the Scots and the cockney, all speak English. And then too, all the countries that was in the empire that the sun never set pon—New Zealand, Australia, Hong Kong, India, Kenya, South Africa, Ghana, Barbados, Jamaica, the United States of America (Boston, New York, Alabama, Texas, Chicago) and Canada, all speak English. Somehow the fact that they all speak different forms of English don't seem to matter.

And what do we say about Chaucer, Shakespeare and the King James version of the Bible? Dialects or language?

Therefore there is no such thing as English Literature as we are still teaching in schools but Literature in English. Of course the first means the literature of England while the second means the literature of the English-speaking world with all its variations and non-standards.

And then lawyers does speak a different form of English than doctors or engineers or computer programmers. And young people does speak a different English than older people who does also speak a different English from older people before them. Ask Al Gilkes where the word 'chossel' come from. Or ask Kitchener where he get 'dingolay' and 'lahay' from.

WILLIAM LABOV

So language is about communication and there is no standard means of communicating between different people, different groups, and different professionals unless one knows the vocabulary and codes and the meaning of the words and the formula of how that language works—the structure.

According to William Labov, Professor of Linguistics at the University of

Pennsylvania, Past President of the Linguistic Society of America and a member of the National Academy of Science: "there is a language, or features of language, common to all people of African ancestry, whether they live in Africa, Brazil or the United States... But it is distinct in many ways, and it is more different from standard English than any other dialect spoken in continental North America. It is not simply slang, or grammatical mistakes, but a well-formed set of rules of pronunciation and grammar that is capable of conveying complex logic and reasoning."

Prof Labov further pointed out that there are two issues confronting teachers and policy makers. The first is that any recognition of a non-standard language as a legitimate means of expression will only confuse children, and reinforce their tendency to use it instead of standard English. The other is that children learn most rapidly in their home language, and that they can benefit in both motivation and achievement by getting a head start in learning to read and write in this way.

There is also agreement that much of the Black American language that Trevor Marshall laments is corrupting us has developed in the last twenty years. There are several books examining the language of rap and dub, the two dominant musical expressions of new world Africans where the imagery, complexity of thought and the word sounds are examined in detail. It is this music

TREVOR MARSHALL

source that spreads the language and reinforces it like steel in concrete.

The Nobel Laureate Toni Morrison said recently: "There are certain things I cannot say without recourse to my language.

It's terrible to think that a child with five different languages comes to school to be faced with books that are less than his own language. And then to be told things about his language, which is him, that are sometimes permanently damaging... This is a really cruel fallout of racism. I know the standard English. I want to use it to restore the other language, the lingua franca."

I would hope that the Ministry of Education and the Faculty of Education would seriously look at what is happening rather than hold on to dated concepts. Language is about communication and we certainly need to strengthen that.

Timothy Callender Remembered

"We also have to take note that, to Africans, a 'person' is really two things, a body and a spirit! or, better yet, a spirit inside, and guiding a body. It was this spirit, or soul, which had the real importance; the body was secondary. When the body died the spirit moved away to the spirit world; when a body was born/conceived, a spirit entered it and completed it, making it a whole 'person'. It was the spirit which guided the body, and while the spirits were thought to be originally good, it was possible for bad spirits to exist through their own systematic practice of disharmony and evil."

Timothy Callender, 'Religion, The Basis of African Culture'

TIMOTHY CALLENDER possessed an amazing intellect. Some would want to use the term intellectual. That he was, but in the context of how he lived his life, I prefer not to use that term. And I'll tell you why.

TIMOTHY
CALLENDER

I first met Timmy through his short stories, his tales of Victoria Village, his surrogate name for every village in Barbados. These stories were culled from the people around him and through them helped to define for me what it was to be Bajan. The fact that he was a young man did not alter the strength of the insights that infused his stories. Nor did the fact that they appeared simple, bar you from understanding that he was providing you with the essence of Bajaness.

In the late sixties he went to Jamaica to study. He came back to

Barbados on vacation and brought with him a young Jamaican artist whose name I don't recall. I posed for them at a house in Brighton. They were both young artists. Both trying their hands at sculpture. It was during this phase that Timmy produced the bust of Barrow that he presented to the Public Library.

Watching Timmy and Jamaica work was a revelation. Timmy was studied and deliberate, always asking questions of himself openly and looking to answer the questions himself. Jamaica, as I called his friend, was intuitive, working much faster and almost from memory taking far fewer looks at me than Timmy.

His friend returned to Jamaica with a dose of gonorrhea and died within seconds of the penicillin shot administered by the doctor. He never knew that he was allergic to penicillin and the doctor never asked nor tested.

Timmy was a searcher, a seeker of truth. He was the perennial imp asking direct questions like a child. Moving in close to you, peeking over his black horn-rimmed glasses, either laughing one minute or serious in the next, with an expression of wonderment at your answer. And when you thought the subject was closed, he reappeared like a recurring decimal with more questions. At the conclusion, his creative mind took over offering some of the most outlandish reasons or scenarios culminating in the raucous laugh that was his trademark.

Like most of us in the sixties, he searched for answers about his own identity and about our collective identity as African people. His own identity was friccaseed when he was kicked out of the Closed Brethren Church, and concomitantly out of his parents' house since they were not permitted to have him in their house; a heavy burden for a teenaged youth which no doubt left invisible scars somewhere under his scalp. That was an ongoing study that never did quite have a concluding answer. But alternatively it led to his explorations into understanding African religiosity.

In Jamaica, he was involved in the student uprising at the UWI (Mona) and the massive sit-in at the then Cultural Arts Centre to protest the banning of Walter Rodney, the Pan-Africanist teacher and historian. Timmy, as a seeker of truth, participated in the protests as an advocate of the teachings of Rodney, but moreso for the experience of being a protestor, a revolutionary, a provocateur. It was the ultimate defiance, a primordial link with the black world that was attempting to redefine itself first at the Bandung Conference and then with the decision by the Supreme Court in the USA that separate education for Blacks was not equal education.

Timmy was a voracious reader of any and everything, but he was never satisfied with the intellectual understanding of what he read. He always wanted to experience it, to match the two sensations. He taught himself to play the guitar so he could compose music for himself to use in his plays rather than use someone's music. He read about mystics drinking their own urine. He felt that the practice of mystics was worth serious consideration and provided a new frontier of experience. He drank his own urine.

Timothy Callender, during his life, explored all manner of experiences: yoga, fasting, sex, drugs, and all the creative art forms. As he gained his insights and understandings, he shared them with his family, his friends and his associates. He was a teacher. He taught us that there was a Nation language, that Bajan English was different from English English and that most people who called for Bajans to use English properly did not even know that what they were calling for was not the English English but Bajan English.

He taught the basic principles of what makes quality art. He never complicated his teachings with complex abstractions, which he was capable of doing, but instead preferred a simplicity that would allow anyone to grasp and understand the meaning of his teachings.

I remember taking him and Tony Lynch, the photographer, with me to visit Black Ben, an African Scientist, at his home just off St. Stephen's Hill, Black Rock. The interior of Black Ben's house was burnt black like if it was charcoal. You could peel off the charred top layer with your fingernail. It was my third visit and Timmy's first. The questions came fast and furious. Black Ben produced a bible and told Timmy to open it at any page and point at any part of the page. Timmy did it and each time Black Ben recited the scriptures under Timmy's fingertips. There was only a small lamp in the corner with its flame dancing precariously on the wick. Not enough for anyone two feet away to read.

Timmy said "no…" "…it was a trick," he said, and he made sure that each time he opened the bible he would turn over a few more pages before he made his selection. Each time Black Ben read the passages from his mind.

ELOMBE INTERVIEWING TIMOTHY CALLENDER

He ordered us to leave his house before dark as he wasn't sure he could protect us from the spirits who came in the house as the sun set. As he explained it, good spirits and bad spirits came to see him every night. He was not sure he could control the bad spirits, so we had to leave.

Black Ben offered us several protection devices consisting of the use of herbs, words and specific rituals. Timmy was the only one who tried them all. One was walking into the sea backwards pausing in the surf, turning a number of times, stopping at each point of the compass, and scrubbing your skin with some herbs which you had to purchase from a woman who sold them in front of the CIVIC building at the corner of Swan, Roebuck and High Streets.

I remember discussing with Timmy an out-of-body experience I had where I saw myself floating about four feet above the bed. I was connected to my body on the bed by a long cord. I don't know how long the experience lasted, it seemed as if it was hours, but it could have been minutes or more likely a few seconds.

Timmy asked if I never saw a light. I said no. Then he explained how he had many such experiences. And he saw lights.

Timmy had purchased several volumes of books from members of the Rosicrucian Order: the Hutchinsons who lived at Windsor Lodge (which the telephone company bought and tore down to build the now existing complex in Government Hill) and Sam Marshall, the veritable kitchen garden farmer from Eckstein Village. From these readings, Timmy explored many aspects of the esoteric sciences and altered states of existence.

Drugs (ganja, cocaine and crack) offered Timmy a shortcut to these altered states and I feel that he experienced many things which he could not explain nor forget. One of these was the light he spoke about. He always seemed to be trying to reach these altered states.

He knew more about drugs than anyone I know. He wrote about cocaine its origins, its uses, and its dangers. Yet he continued to use coke and crack again and again in pursuit of his elusive states of mind.

As the intensity of his experience grew, it caused him to neglect his family and discard material things with a vengeance. It is easy for many to say that he was a drug addict. Maybe he was, but I certainly felt he discovered something that he wanted to match back to his intellectual and experiential understanding and he was prepared to follow it. He gave up his life for it.

Timmy used to teach that Europe mastered technology in order to control the material/physical world while Africa used magic to control the spiritual world. Maybe he found his magic.

Broodie: My Hero

DEAR BROODIE:

I don't know if you knew a lady by the name of Elsie Holder. She was a teacher at Eagle Hall Primary School, in the back of Black Rock, really Goodland. Yuh had was to go through a little gap in front Dr. Roberts' house to reach the one-room board and shingle building. At least that is the road we used to take to get to school.

Miss Holder was as tall as you; a little buxom, with nuff freckles or moles pon she face. Like you she lived in a chattel-house. Hers was situated in The Kew Road, Tudor Bridge, pon de downside of the road in the middle of Kew Hill.

It is Miss Holder I have to thank for introducing me to you. I know that you may not know her and that in reality she never really introduced me to you. But she was the first person that taught me how to draw and paint. As a little boy I used to sit on her gallery and draw chattel-houses, learning how to get the perspectives right and how to use water colour. She taught me how to make kites too and to play the notes and scales on the piano which she played.

Miss Holder was an unusual woman for her time and she migrated to the UK after taking an early retirement.

From those lessons I encountered you and Ivan Payne at the Annual Agricultural Exhibition in Queen's Park.

I remember asking my father bout you and he tell me that you helped Freddie Miller (Billie's father) build an airplane that never got off the ground. Later in the sixties you had me in hysterics with the full story of that enterprise in your studio above Walkes Drug Store in Tudor Street.

You were still living in the house over in Seclusion where it was said you were an obeah man who could turn into a duck at night. In the fifties I would be extremely careful when I pass your house pon my bicycle going to Jack-Muh-Nanny Gap (Wavell Avenue).

I remember how attached you were to the house in Seclusion and were reluctant to part with it after your son Virgil bought you the big house in Strathclyde. But it was there that you assembled the work that reflected your life: your sculpture, your paintings, your collection of art by others, your collection of slides and photographs of all sorts of exhibitions, your collection of art reviews, the works of your students. It was there with you and Eunice that I listened to the stories of hardship, of unacceptance, of struggle to sell one little piece of work from your little gallery in Pelican Village.

It was at Strathclyde that I first saw the sculpture that I called Bussa. It was a commission by the government of Guyana to represent Cuffy, the slave leader. I remember getting your permission to use it as the symbol for the BUSSA Awards in 1972 and promising to see that it was erected in Barbados. I did, but was never invited to the unveiling.

I remember the Gary Sobers and the Frank Worrell

BUSSA

commissions (and the models) implemented by the government of Barbados, only to be voided by indecision. Then there was Grantley Adams. You talked about his big head and the way in which he held it and what was the optimum size for such a sculpture. And the authorities waited so long that the model collapsed. And then they called, desperate. "No," you said. You were sick, so sick you couldn't receive the Doctorate that the University of the West Indies conferred on you.

There was talk of getting Adams made in Guyana or Jamaica or God knows where. I said no, that is Broodie's to do. And so when I asked you to do something as monumental as a public sculpture of Grantley Adams at your age (88 years) in such a short time even though you were not in the best of health, you agreed to with the help of Virgil. I knew then how great you are.

Again, I was not invited to the unveiling of your most recent work.

Although Virgil and Eunice were towers of strength for you to finish the Adams in such a short time, I would hope that the government of Barbados and the University of the West Indies act now in giving you the commissions for the production of Garfield Sobers and Frank Worrell respectively.

I salute you with your two public sculptures and possibility of two more. There is no one like you in this Caribbean of ours. You are indeed a national treasure and a hero.

Broodie, you are indeed a Master. You are my own special hero.

Karl Broodhagen, the Master

QUEEN'S PARK used to be the venue for the Annual Agriculture and Industrial Exhibition. It used to run for two days. It was held in December close to Christmas and it was the place that you had to go. It was a ritual, a rite of passage. It was the place where you wore your first long pants. It was the place where you established your first rendezvous with someone of the opposite sex. You met all your friends under the clock at the top of the front of the maintenance building.

KARL BROODHAGEN

Queen's Park was zoned. The Gymkhana was held on the Spartan pasture. The perimeter had the stock pens with the cows and sheep and goats and pigs and other large animals. The feathered stock was in the Steel Shed—every variety of yard fowl, cellar duck and sky bird. Furniture and craft were ensconced in the Queen's Park, both upstairs and downstairs. And in the Stables at the back were the art exhibitions.

It was here in the Stables that I first saw the works of Ivan Payne and Karl Broodhagen.

Karl Broodhagen, the man with the strange name who came originally from BG with his mudda. Yes, BG, sometimes Demerara or Berbice. That's what my mudda used to call the present-day Guyana.

I was fascinated with the paintings I used to see at these exhibitions. The only other names I could remember were Kathleen Hawkins and Elsie Holder, a woman from the Kew who used to teach art at Eagle Hall Primary School in Goodland where I went to school. She used to teach me music and art. She did tell me where Karl Broodhagen lived over in Seclusion, Black Rock.

Besides the three Ws, my heroes were Ivan Payne and Karl Broodhagen. But like all heroes, they never knew. Ivan Payne was from Speightstown, where my mudda did come from. But I could only see he work at the Exhibition. The same ting with Karl Broodhagen's work.

Late in 1966, I established contact with these two idols of mine. It soon became a passion to bring them to the general public. I was determined to mount two major one-man exhibitions to highlight the work of each master. Ivan Payne's was held during the seventies at the Bank of America on Lower Broad Street under the auspices of Yoruba and Karl Broodhagen's was held in the Queen's Park Gallery under the auspices of the National Cultural Foundation.

I spent a lot of time with Broodie at his studio above Walkes Drugstore in Lower Baxter's Road, just above where Milk Market ended, and then at his Pelican Gallery in Pelican Village. It was in these surroundings that I encountered Broodie the raconteur.

I heard first-hand the stories of Everton Football Club and the Reef, of Frank Walcott and Freddie Miller, of the beautiful women of the city, of ballroom dancing, of boxing, of Sal (my Uncle Llewellyn) who was a tailor like he, Broodie.

He tell me bout Freddie Miller and Butcher who built the first airplane in Barbados. How they put in a lorry engine and how he Broodie make the skin of the plane with some special cloth. He

ELOMBE OPENING BROODHAGEN EXHIBITION
AT QUEEN'S PARK GALLERY

even show me a piece of the cloth that was left over. I think the plane was to take off from the Garrison, but it never did. I forget what happened.

And as Broodie talked, he would be working on a piece of sculpture that he knew nobody was going to buy, but he had to do it nevertheless.

And like the boxer he was, his pointing finger would be jabbing the air or jabbing your chest as the stories uncurled from his lips, animated by his sparkling eyes and punctuated by a joyous laugh, or a bob and weave chupse of disapproval of the actions of one of the characters in his stories.

Broodie was a teacher, not only of art, but of life. Not only in the classroom where he spent nearly sixty years, but outside where he nurtured every aspiring artist.

Over the years, Broodie maintained records and he has documented almost every art exhibition held in Barbados. His records are replete with newspaper clippings, photographs and slides, brochures and catalogues of art in Barbados for the last fifty years at least.

In addition there are endless notebooks of sketches of real and imaginary characters and personalities in Barbados. His sculpture is a 'who is who' of Barbados over the last half-century.

And yet without reward or commissions, he continued his work with an incessant drive based on his love of people and his love for his art.

In the early seventies, when I established the Bussa Awards, Karl Broodhagen was one of the first recipients. Except for the British Council Scholarship he received to study art in the UK, it was the only recognition from this his adopted country.

At that award ceremony held at the Centre for Multi-Racial Studies, I persuaded him to display the statue that I christened Bussa. I gave him the assurance then that I would see that it was erected in Barbados. The opportunity came in 1983, and it stands at the roundabout at Two Mile Hill reflecting the emancipation of our people from the bondage of slavery, both as slaves and masters.

Broodie has given to Barbados a treasury of creativity that cannot be matched by anyone living or dead. It certainly would take as remarkable a man to match his output and single-mindedness. I trust that the Barbados government and the people of Barbados will recognize the monumental legacy he is leaving to us. I hope that they will take the necessary action to maintain intact this legacy and to preserve it for future generations. It must not be allowed to be scattered hither, thither and yon.

Broodie celebrates his eighty-eighth birthday on July 4. In October, this venerable Master Sculptor will be awarded an Honorary Doctorate by the University of the West Indies, Cave Hill.

Karl Broodhagen is a humble man, but he is not an ordinary man. Karl Broodhagen is a man of awesome talent and vision. He possesses an energy that has infected all those who have been his friends, his students and his audience.

Happy Birthday, Broodie. Your work will never end.

Smokey and the Festival Band

THERE IS nothing like a sour akee that does tie up yuh tongue in knots, not just any knot but dem fine knots dat when yuh pickin dem is like yuh pickin black cobbler prickles from yuh foot. Nothing, except of course a sour note played by a musician in the middle of a kaiso.

Most of the time in a live performance, most people don't hear dem sour-akee notes. At least their minds don't linger long pon dat note but become distracted by the performance, the time and the place.

However, when the performance is recorded and you hear dat sour akee note, dog nyam yuh supper. It spile up the whole song.

And so this was the state of calypso in 1982. Real akee notes in the tents because most of the musicians were mekking sport. Many of the instruments were out of tune. There were few meaningful arrangements. There were no standards or commitment to anything called a standard.

The two radio stations, CBC and Rediffusion, used to organize separate recordings with the tents on different nights. The product they got was generally bad. Usually two discordant versions full of sour akee notes bringing the whole art form into disrepute. Tek dem off the air! Ban dem! The criticisms in 1980 were relentless.

In 1982, I was invited by the Ministry of Information and Culture to produce Crop Over. I was then Director of Productions at CBC Radio. Before agreeing to produce Crop

Over, I ordered 200 five-minute tape carts for my department. A major criticism from the calypsonians themselves was that only certain people used to get their songs played. The truth was that any discrimination that existed had to do with the fact that most of the recordings were on seven-inch tapes or even longer, and this made retrieval difficult. Each calypso was to be placed on a five-minute cart. Carts recue themselves to the start. This made it easy for an operator or DJ to access the songs.

The only tent band that had any semblance of quality was the House of Soca band lead by Smokey Roett. In that band was also the cream of the Police Band. Most importantly, most of the musicians in the House of Soca band could read music, and

SMOKEY ROETT

therefore rehearsals were shorter and the output was usually better.

The Ministry of Information and Culture had inherited a host of sound equipment that was purchased for hosting CARIFESTA. A large part of that equipment was available for Crop Over. We took the decision to record all the tents and provide a single quality product to the radio stations and CBC-TV. You would hear one version of a song no matter which radio station you listened to or watched. That was the year of *Jack* and *Mr. Harding Can't Burn*.

At the tent recordings, no taping was accepted if the instruments were out of tune. Roger Gibbs and then Hal Archer had the responsibility to make sure that this took place. It was written into the contract with the tents that this was a requirement for being recorded.

ROGER GIBBS

Usually each tent had its own backing band, and the quality varied widely depending on the quality of the tent's management.

HAL ARCHER

Again we took another decision. All persons selected for the semi-finals had to have arrangements because we would have only one band on stage, the Festival Band, which would be made up of the best musicians in Barbados. Best also meant they would have to be able to read music. They were also going to be paid top dollars. Every performer was therefore placed on a level playing field.

In order to assist the calypsonians, we agreed to pay for all of the arrangements of persons selected for the semifinals. The choice of arranger was theirs. This agreement was for three years. After that, calypsonians had to pay for their own arrangements for Waterford. The effect of this decision was that calypsonians started getting arrangements done before Crop Over opened and used them in the tents, thus improving the quality of the tents and the subsequent recorded performances.

Perhaps the most significant achievement, though, was the performance of the Festival Band under the leadership of Smokey Roett. It was Smokey who kept the band on an even keel throughout the years. His was not an easy task, as there were a rebellious lot from time to time. But Smokey persevered and always extracted from the band some amazing performances.

The idea of the Festival Band did not go down well with most calypsonians. It was something new and we were taking them out of their comfort zone. It is important to remember that most calypsonians were not singers. They were performers who used what they had to put over a song. Many had lousy voices. The most important thing, though, was that they had heart and took their art form seriously.

The use of an arranger was a given once the Festival Band concept was implemented and that is why we undertook to fund this expense for three years to bridge the gap between what was and what the future demanded.

In determining the size and shape of the band, I was influenced by the sounds of the Duke Ellington and Count Basie bands. From Duke's band came the sweetness of the saxes with the boisterous baritone sax anchoring that section. From Count came the sparkling precise crisp brass and their aerobatic punctuations. Underlying all of this was a rhythm section that defined the tempo and drove the whole performance forward.

The Festival Band was not just about backing the calypsonians at Crop Over, it was a vehicle to provide an opportunity for our top musicians to demonstrate their capacity to perform in a disciplined way. It was also a vehicle for writers and arrangers to display ideas that had their gestation in their music studies.

In the early years of the band, the arrangers took full advantage of the size and range of its instrumentation. A great deal of quality musicianship went into the backing of the calypsonians.

Listen to Gabby's *Calypso* recorded at the Pic-O-De-Crop Finals in 1982. This is not just a classic as a composition, but the voicings, the harmonies, the sharp razor-edged brass and the percolating rhythm, cutting this way then changing direction, syncopating like a hiccup, matches Gabby's phrasing and masterful performance. I believe it was Mike Sealy who did this arrangement. The band was on and Smokey was in command.

Over the years, arrangers failed to fully capitalize on the structure of the Band. Many got slack and lazy and failed to produce arrangements that really challenged the band. Again,

MIKE SEALY

Mike Sealy has perhaps been the most consistent and imaginative of all the arrangers, excelling with his work for Invader #3, for example.

The last performance of the Festival Band under Smokey was in 1998, and there is no doubt that it was one of their greatest, if not their greatest, performances. The conditions and sound mixing were excellent. Many times the sound mix at the National Stadium and on the air left a lot to be desired. But that year there is no doubt that the Festival Band was at its best under excellent conditions. Listen to its work behind nearly all the calypsonians: Gabby, John King, Kid Site, TC, Kinky Starr and Red Plastic Bag. An awesome performance. And perhaps a fitting epitaph for Smokey and the Festival Band.

In the late 1980s when Bumba sang *Three Blind Mice*, he was afraid to perform it at the Pic-o-de-Crop Finals the way it was recorded. His reasons were really perceptions. First, that the judges would not accept the song and secondly, that the Festival Band would have been offended because he did not have a 'big band' arrangement for them to play.

Three Blind Mice represented to me what the young studio producers were beginning to do. Eddy Grant seemed to be influential in this development. Rhythm was the essential ingredient. Horns were optional and used only if necessary. Lots of synthesizers allowing for a more flexible programmed performance and matching the soundscape of a younger generation.

With the introduction of contemporary interpretations of traditional Bumbatuk rhythms, the Festival Band's vulnerability surfaced. I am not speaking about an inability to play and interpret the music, but the audience had moved to a different level and thus we saw diminishing returns for the abundance of horns. Moreover, the record producers, singers and bands have established a pre-eminence that makes it futile to persist with the Festival Band as is. It was only a matter of time. That time has come. One regret I have is that the band was never recorded in its own right.

I hope that the NCF and the Ministry of Culture will make every effort to produce a CD with the best tunes during its existence so that posterity will have documentation of one of the greatest bands that Barbados has produced.

To Smokey and all the members of the Festival Band, including all those who were members at one time or another, my profound thanks for showing that quality does matter, and for leaving a mark on Barbados' musical history that can never be erased.

Silence and Acquiescence

LOUIS LYNCH was a wit. A dry wit. As dry as the harmattan that collects the Sahara dust and deposits it across the Caribbean. One Sunday morning he was entertaining on his verandah a young man of humble origin whom he thought was a rising political star. He offered the young man a drink, and his wife Marjorie brought out a brand new bottle of Courvoisier and a pair of brandy snifters.

LOUIS LYNCH

He poured the two drinks and before he could say "cheers," the young man tossed back his head and downed the brandy, wiping his mouth with the back of his hand as he skin-up he face. Without batting an eye, Louis shouted out. "Marjorie, bring the rum bottle, I have a rum drinker out here!"

The young man, in his 'progress', had not acquired the socialization that is associated with this European custom, but he was an expert and authority on the cultural norms of Bajans, especially the consumption of rum in rumshops.

Louis Lynch was not a malicious man and his request was not meant to be so, and the rum bottle never did come out as his wife knew him very well. But this story lays bare one of the major problems facing Barbados after Independence. To what extent are we to discard our way of life in the face of foreign cultural practices and how much value should we put on our own cultural expression?

Cultures that have refused to absorb foreign influences have died or dwindled into abject poverty. So I understand the necessity and importance of renewal through an openness to foreign cultures. However, the very essence of what makes us different is what we have developed over the years and which is under serious threat as the century closes.

My first major confrontation with this concept was when I looked at the arts in Barbados just after Independence. The founding and establishment of the Barbados National Theatre Workshop raised quite a number of questions. The most important of these was the paucity of plays about ourselves. We had few indigenous playwrights. Then there was the question of language and its use as a voice for our aspirations. This voice and the cadence of our speech was absent to a large degree from every art form. And then too, the language of movement, of attitude and posture.

There was a lot of difficulty in getting people to accept themselves. How did traditional dance, for example, encapsuled and embodied in the Landship Movement, become representative of a collective memory of an African past and a Bajan present? What was it that caused a man and/or a woman, to dance the dance they danced to a Tuk Band in front a rum shop or on a pasture at an outing or on the streets at Christmas time? What was it that prevented us from displaying it on stage or at any important ritual or event?

We are still struggling with these questions after thirty-three years, as is evidenced by Trevor Marshall's analysis of NIFCA and the persistent criticisms about 'wuk-up' culture. The creativity that is ours to express must be given equality across the board in every art form. Not only in composing and performing popular music or choreography, but in every area of expression, like what the visual artists are free to do and do in fact do.

Over the years we have made ourselves feel that to dance the way we do is to be vulgar. We rip our dance to shreds because of the conflict between the acquired Euro/Christian values (i.e., its whiteness with its inherent implication of superiority) and our own traditions. Our traditions by and large came out of Africa and that is why at Yoruba we brought in teachers to show us the linkages with that very noble tradition. We are yet to establish for dance the same aesthetics we have given to our chattel houses and our cricketing style. It requires nothing more and nothing less.

And you know why we have not and cannot. We look to Europe for approval. We are yet to understand our collective consciousness of being black in a world that keeps telling us that it has no value. We are still struggling to be something other than ourselves. And what we have the world wants, but we are yet to learn how to sell it to the world. There is a saying that the same knife that stick sheep can stick goat. We know that we are yet sleeping or playing petty politics with our lives and the lives of our children.

We are hearing the song "Globalization" and if we are not careful it will be our swan song. Globalization is nothing more than the Americanization of the world. From the day the first movie was produced and made accessible to the world this American/ Globalization process has been taking place. Television and the internet have accentuated this process which is now being followed by political and institutional consolidation. But note there is some resistance.

The greatest resistance to enslavement is our mental resolve and the strength of building ourselves into a formidable force of resistance. Dependency presents itself in many ways and excuses with justification can be found to perpetuate it. Our strength is who we are, what we are and the uniqueness of what happened on this little rock. We must avoid the trap of silence and acquiescence.

When Banja Play, People Come

When Banja Play, People Come

THE SOUNDS of Banja have a habit of fading into your consciousness like how the glow of morning light does burn your eyelids. First it is the flute, like a long-tail Dr. Booby, dancing on the air from over there or over here or somewhere. And then like a chorus of blackbirds chattering on a galvanize roof, in comes the kittie snare with its buzzing after-burn, sparkling wet chrysanthemums of rhythms. And in the bottom of your belly, cradling your heartbeat, you discover the bum drum, echoing in the swallow of your hips.

My response to Banja music was and has always been genetic. Socialization was not a reason since respectability could not accept Banja, that most African of Bajan musics, because it was low-class, non-music performed by low-class people outside rum-shops.

Yet this music that found favour at bus outings and excursions on bank-holidays, at fairs and exhibitions accompanying Maypole dancers and wooden-horse riders, and outside your house on Saturday nights, was deprecated because it was not European or specifically English in its origins.

None of its performers studied at the Royal conservatories or academies. Many could not read a note of music. A few may have been exposed to the sol-fa melodies of village choirs or the rum-laced harmonies of Singings. And this certainly was not enough to give Banja respectability.

"Don't sing any Banja in this house and not at all pon a

Sunday!" That was the cry stifling genetic responses across this island. But when Banja plays, Bajans always come out to see, to laugh and to dance.

When I speak about the swallow of the hips, I am speaking about the natural response that comes from the hips. It is almost as if the music enters your hips from a gulp and ignites an engine. The soles of your feet plant themselves apart. Your knees bend, your back arches, and your hips latch on to the Bumbatuk. Wuk up time!

In the late 1960s, I first met the Benn Hill Sports Band from Mile-and-a-Quarter and recorded them on the beach at Lower Carlton, St. James. The 'Sports' in the band's name comes from ascribing all non-work activity as sport. I was deemed a madman when I played this music on CBC radio.

At Yoruba Yard, we concentrated on exposing many young people to Banja music as performed by the Bumbatuk bands. My original choreography of the Landship for the Yoruba People still remains the definitive stage performance. And the Landship Movement remains a living repository of the traditional dance movements used in dancing to Banja.

Some people see these traditional dance movements as just wukking up. This is not so. The dance movements to Banja need to be analyzed, evaluated and reproduced in new and additional contexts to raise the value and respect for the tradition. Perceptions of lewdness can be eliminated through careful ritualization of the dance process.

Crop Over has allowed some of these dance elements that were under pressure of annihilation before Independence to become part of the popular expression. This should give young choreographers an opportunity to sift this traditional vernacular in Bajan dance to evolve a comparative contemporary idiom to match what has been taking place in Bajan music.

The success of Bajan music in the last four or five years has to do with the incorporation of Bumbatuk rhythms into the contemporary music. Many people think of it as Calypso or Soca music, but it is neither. It is Banja.

On my radio programmes in Jamaica, Jamaicans recognize the difference between Bajan music and Trinidad Soca music and Soca music in general. When I play Bajan music, especially those that capture the Bumbatuk music, what I call Banja, the response is immediate. This has been particularly so since the Bajan Invasion of 1995.

The differences are so clear that I wonder why our producers, our performers and the NCF have failed to capitalize on marketing our music as Banja music or Bajan Banja. Labelling gives a product a separate identity. Labelling has already given Crop Over a separate identity. Why not the music? In this crowded world of entertainment, identity counts. We have identity, let's use it.

When Banja play, people come.

Sweet Sweet Tuk Band Music, Part I

THE FRONT-HOUSE at Merton in Tudor Bridge was made of board, and the gallery at the front was also made of board. The middle part and the back part were also made of board. The only parts that were wall were the bedroom and the verandah pon de side with the garden.

You could only get to the house from the public road by coming up a driveway with a little hill. The driveway was pon de other side of the house. And from the driveway there were two steps that carried you up to the house steps.

It was when they were shuffling and scuffling up the steps that we would hear them. Next you would hear de scraping pon the side of the house as if somebody was trying to brek in. And soon you would feel the floor vibrate like if it is a earthquake.

In no time we would be out of our beds running through the front house to the gallery to peep through the flaps or the glass windows. We knew the sounds. We used to hear them at Easter, at Whitsun, pon de King's Birthday, pon Civic Day (New Year's Day) and every other bank holiday.

Or pon a Sarduh night, when dum passing the house coming from Eagle Hall gine to Louis Piggott shop at the corner of Fairfield in front the Kew Road, followed by a crowd like a Easter kite tail waggin bout behind dem.

But Christmas was different. Dat is when dem gine sing and beg fuh rum and sorrell and Christmas cake and sweet bread and something salt like ham. Dat is when dem gun lick cork pon the drum. Dat is when the music really start to play.

A Bajan Tuk band... my first love.

I regret I don't know the names of the many anonymous players who I heard in those days. Sometimes they came in fours or fives or more. Bum, kittie, triangle and flute. And sometimes there may be a guitar, a banjo, a shak-shak, a jawbone of an ass or more likely a cow, a bottle, a shookster, or bread-paper and comb, which added all kinds of combinations.

A shookster was a barrel stave with a taut, tuned wire running from one end to the next. It was plucked like a mudda fiddle while it rested on the side of a board house. The house acted as the resonator. It was the shookster that vibrated the house.

The shookster may have been unique to Barbados, but it is similar in conception to many traditional African instruments of the same ilk. For example, the wash-tub bass used in the Southern United States among African-Americans is a similar device. So too is the box-bass (rumba-box in Jamaica, marimbula in parts of Latin America), or the earth-bow (a bent stick with a cord attached to an animal skin covering a hole in the ground).

At christmas especially, Tuk Bands were accompanied by Tiltmen, Donkey Belly, Dancing Bears and other masked dancers with cock hats. And there were always singers with their rhymes of solicitation for food and/or money.

I cannot recall ever seeing any of these groups visit our house in daylight, although I have seen them at the Annual Agricultural Exhibition and on Civic Day in Queen's Park, and at outings in the country. But it was always at night during the christmas season. Close to midnight or after that they came to the house. Theirs was an all-night journey going from house to house and time was therefore irrelevant.

We always had the rum and glasses ready for the invasion.

Ham and pork cutters were also available along with sorrel, ginger beer and other drinks.

I want to look at these Tuk Bands, starting with the flute players.

The first Tuk Band musician that I knew by name was a tall 'red' man who used to sell Barbados Turf Club tickets. He carried the tickets in a bag hanging from his shoulder so that his hands were free. His name was Duplex and he was forever playing a flute.

He was what you would call a flute virtuoso—a solo player who learnt his art in his youth in a Tuk Band. He had a fluid style, the hallmark of which was his nimble fingers. He was not a showman, and his elegant style was in many ways controlled by his business of sweepstakes ticket selling. He attracted his customers like a town crier, his flute was his megaphone. Duplex was the master from which all others are to be judged.

Joe Cadogan of the Benn Hill Sports Band from Mile-and-a-Quarter, St. Peter, was unique in that he didn't use the usual tin flute, but the wooden body of an old clarinet. This resulted in a mellow sound which resonated with harmonics not heard in traditional Tuk Bands.

Benn Hill Sports Band was not just an instrumental Tuk Band, but a singing band that recalled the songs of the pre-technological days. Joe Cadogan, like a Barney Bigard or a Sidney Bechet, complimented the singer with choice comments and supplemental runs on his unique flute.

Luckily, I have been able to record this band for posterity.

Sweet Sweet Tuk Band Music, Part II

THE CIVIC Friendly Society at one time had a membership of over 40,000 people. For nearly three decades, the first day of the year was known and celebrated as Civic Day. Tuk Bands were always there playing for the Wooden Horse (Merry-go-Round), Maypole, the Landship or masqueraders.

We continue our look at the Tuk Band and some of its outstanding players.

Another fine flute player was Poui, with his twisted, contorted body stylings. Knees bent to form an X, elbows tucked tightly into his ribs, head moving rapidly from side to side or up and down like a suspicious blackbird, Poui expressed the fire of green rum, the green rum that stunned his throat into submission to provide the spitfire melody lines from his flute, his glazed eyes and tied tongued unbalancing him with each movement. His appearance with numerous Tuk Bands indicates his commitment to his art.

POUI

The great Seaman, the modernist, was the fearless explorer of contemporary sounds. I don't know how he got his name but when he plays, I can't help but feel a strong connection with the so-called Tradewinds, the formidable winds that fuelled the African slave trade, that dispersed the anguished and painful cries of helpless sufferers. A superb stylist, confident to the point of arrogance about his powerful playing.

SEAMAN

Seaman is a man who understands the tradition by living it and creating it up front. So confident is he that he introduced the alto sax as an alternate voice to allow him to access with greater ease the contemporary songs he hears. Like Duplex, his music is part of his job, always at hand, to practise, to play whenever there was a moment to be claimed. Many travellers on the Transport Board buses can attest to this. He has influenced a whole new generation of flute players.

POONKA

Poonka is the consummate musicologist/performer. He brings a profound understanding of the place of Bumbatuk music in the cultural heritage of Barbados. He has not just mastered the flute, but all the instruments: the drums and the assorted percussion instruments, as well as the vernacular of music as has been expressed in his calypsoes. It has taken arrangers over a decade to master what he clearly understood years ago and what we tried to introduce in the years after Independence in 1966.

His intellect, sensitivity and sensibility has helped to elevate this traditional music of ours to national and international recognition. His analyses and documentation of the tradition are unsurpassed and continue to encourage both traditional players and contemporary interpreters.

Although I have so far concentrated on the flute players, this traditional music of ours that was so readily accessible in the past as I have described above, was always driven by the rhythms of the supporting drums, the Kittie and the Bum.

These rhythms survived the censorship of the plantocratic laws through a series of cutting and contriving acts; of camouflaging rhythmic patterns within the march and the waltz. The advent of the Landship Movement in 1865 legitimized the continual use of these rhythms.

SON SON BISHIP

In our time, besides the sterling work of Poonka and his young contemporaries, two drummers stand out—Son-Son Bishop and Potato Mout.

Son-Son Bishop was an Oistins-based fisherman who picked up the tradition of drumming as a youngster when King George and the Dragon was still being performed up by Aberdeen Jones shop pon top of Oistins's Hill, and when sticklicking was still the sport of men.

Son-Son Bishop enjoyed his playing and this could be seen in his body language and the spirit that infused his playing. He was always in control, always pushing, kicking up dust like he playing for a wooden horse or stoking the engine of a Landship on manoeuvres.

In contrast, Potato Mout, whose nickname is derived from the shape of his mouth and the sourness of his face, is a study of concentration while he is playing. Here is a man whose art was not just in his playing but in the construction of the

POTATO MOUT

221

drums, from selecting the material for the bodies to the hoops to the rings to the goat skins and to the designs on the outside.

He was thoroughly respectful of the process, of how the drums were to be made, when they could be made and for whom. They could not be rushed and everything had to be done right. He would not waste time making drums for anyone he had contempt for… and that included most of the world.

As a Kittie drummer, he possessed a fantastic sense of timing, the essence of the best drummers. His dynamic level was subtle and pervasive, responding continuously to Seaman's flute and the controlling Bum drum. He never faltered or lost a beat and the sweeter he played the more sour his face became. Yet for all of this, his body was always supple and relaxed, allowing him to deliver his rolls, cuts and explosive bombs like a mongoose in a chicken coop. When he pumping he pumping.

We take for granted this traditional music of ours. It is fragile and is dependent on solid and unwavering support from those who respect our heritage and what it means to be Bajan. We are faced with very powerful contemporary music forms from our neighbours, near and far. It is our link to the past when such music was as commonplace as the air we breathe. Let us keep this sweet, sweet music alive for our children's children.

Bumbatuk Music and Calypso I

WITHIN A month after Barbados got its Independence in 1966, I set about a search to discover who or what is a Bajan. In the next three years, I travelled every single paved road and about 50 percent of the existing cart roads in Barbados at least once.

I walked through every major gully, along most of the beaches and followed the old railway line along its legendary path from River Road to Muh Lady's Passage above Consett Bay, St. John.

This search was not only to learn the landscape, but to discover our people, their language and the rhythms of their life. It is a search that is yet to end, and every day brings discovery, a revelation of something new and different.

One of the cultural elements that caught my attention was the Barbados Landship Movement. I believe I visited every existing ship at its Dock from Rose Hill, Mile-and-a-Quarter, St. Peter to Merricks in St. Phillip.

This exploration of the Landship was two-fold: firstly, to examine the organization, its structure, practices and functions; and secondly, to explore the Bumbatuk music used by the Landships when they were holding manoeuvres.

Bumbatuk music existed independently of the Landship. It has a long history and parallels the presence of Africans from their earliest days in Barbados.

I spent a long time talking and/or recording the likes of Potato Mout and Seaman and Son Son Bishop and many other nameless stalwarts who propelled the Landships or entertained the rum-drinking patrons of urban and country rumshops on Saturdays.

I grew up in Tudor Bridge/Eagle Hall listening every Saturday night to Bumbatuk Bands (and Village Choirs at christmas time.)

The fascinating thing about Tuk Bands was that besides the Bum Drum and the Kittie and the Penny Whistle/fife, the Tuk Band could be expanded to include triangle or bones or banjo/guitar or shak-shak or bread-paper and comb or even saxophone.

A regular feature about the Bumbatuk Bands of my childhood was that singing was a major part of the group's performance. Today's bands tend to be more instrumental.

In the late 1960s, it was rare to find a band that still did both, but I did find one. It was the Benn Hill Sports Band. (Sports was a name given to making of music and dancing.) Although Benn Hill is an area in Mile-and-a-Quarter, I recorded them one day on the beach in Lower Carlton, St. James.

The Penny Whistle used in the group was an old wooden clarinet body converted to serve the same purpose, giving a mellower sound than the original instrument. But more importantly, the flute player sang lead on all the songs as well. The singing was full of speech rhythms. The phrasing was unlike anything I had heard before. The rhythms on the drums and triangle were complementary, accenting the melody line of both the voice and the flute.

As a member of the Barbados Arts Council with responsibility for their radio program on CBC Radio 900, I attempted to play the tape of this group. I was promptly reported to the Program Manager for playing "a bunch of noise and foolishness." Needles to say, I insisted and succeeded in breaking the barrier that had been erected against this music.

This recording of the Benn Hill Sports Band became a major inspiration as I worked at Yoruba Yard introducing these cultural elements to the young people of Barbados. I had already introduced some of this material to the Modern High School and subsequently at a public performance at the Barbados Museum.

At first, I attempted to bring the authentic original artists (Potato Mout, Son Son Bishop, et al.) on to the stage at Yoruba Yard. I encountered a major difficulty. Traditional artists are accustomed to performing in a context that has no end. The audience drifts into the visual and aural circle and when it has had enough, drifts away again. The traditional artists continue to play.

In the theatrical setting of a stage and a sitting audience, it is the performers who must complete their performance and move away. Traditional artists found great difficulty in meeting this requirement. It was necessary to train and develop artists who had the understanding and capability to perform in such a setting.

This also led to the development of the adjunct masquerade expressions such as Shaggy Bear, Donkey Belly, and Tiltman among others. Many of these forms were therefore introduced at Yoruba Yard in an artistic context to demonstrate the core music of Bajan culture.

What many people still don't recognize or want to recognize is that there are dance forms that belong to this vernacular musical expression. Wukking up is one such movement, but not the only one. I have pointed out elsewhere that the Landship is a repository of these dance forms.

For many years the Eurocentric bias of our education foisted on us a value system that deprecated our indigenous expressions. As such, much of this music was labelled Banja (meaning African-oriented music) and deemed unacceptable. Our work at Yoruba Yard was to dispel these views and demonstrate our own links to a long tradition in Africa.

Two Africans from Nigeria, el Verno del Congo and several

EL VERNO DEL CONGO GROUP 1975

Bumbatuk drummers, worked with us at Yoruba Yard to help us develop a cadre of drummers. We developed a number of outstanding drummers who became the 'engine room' of the Yoruba People, the performing group at Yoruba Yard. Two of those outstanding drummers were Wayne Willock and Ifie, the percussionist with Spice, who first learnt walking on stilts and drumming at Yoruba Yard.

Wayne Willock comes from a very musical family. His father, Ernest Willock, played the Mudda Fiddle (string bass) in Percy Green's Band and was the last leader of that aggregation before it was disbanded. Steeped in church music, his father and his mother were also major players in the Barbados Folk Singers. His younger brother is also a percussionist.

Next week I want to look at the conversion of Wayne Willock to Poonka and his entry into calypso.

Bumbatuk Music and Calypso II

WAYNE WILLOCK is one of those rare individuals in Barbados who has been able to combine his intellectualism, his language skills, and his original research into a performance vehicle. That vehicle is his calypso personality called Poonka.

In *Tuk Band Rhythm*, his seminal tune, he not only captures the essence of the tradition, but he incorporates musical and lyrical phrases from some of these traditional songs into his composition.

What marks this particular composition is the use of the 'cream-o-wheat' flute phrase as the opening gambit for the tune. It is a bold declaration that captures the tradition and declares Poonka's understanding and commitment to the tradition.

He defines all aspects of the Tuk band, its instrumentation, its function and the context in which it was likely to be found.

Within the calypso competition, however, *Tuk Band Rhythm* and several of his other compositions fall short of what I would call the modernization of Tuk rhythm or Bumbatuk. The reasons are quite simple and obvious.

Poonka's performances fall within a Crop Over Festival that was attempting to define itself as a celebration of what is Bajan. At its core, as with any harvest, is a celebration of nature, a traditional practice that is found throughout the world. Crop Over has its origins both in Africa and in Europe.

However, it is important to recognize that Africa's rhythm is the powerful engine that drives this festival regardless of whatever other elements which may also have been incorporated into it from other cultures. These African rhythms have also gained a distinctive character in this environment, in this island called Barbados. Conditions were created within which our Tuk developed.

But all of these developments were taking place in a musical tradition that put a great deal of emphasis on European harmonies and structure. Not just because of the music, but because of its promotion as superior to the traditions of Africa.

Thus arrangers and calypsonians continued to stick close to the traditional calypso rhythms, structured for acceptance in the twentieth century Caribbean. Even Poonka allowed his conga playing to pre-empt (on several occasions) his Tuk band rhythms. (Check out all the arguments about what is or isn't calypso etc.)

The prevailing music of Barbados in terms of contemporary sounds has been calypso from Trinidad, American Rhythm and Blues and the musics of Jamaica (Ska, Reggae and Dancehall).

POONKA TUK BAND ON THE ROAD

These sounds are important in the sense that they have influenced and will continue to influence the evolution of Bajan music. These inputs keep the Bajan musical culture dynamic and alive.

However, whenever all is said and done, the core of what constitutes Bajan musical tradition is what will sustain and identify us as Bajan. Poonka understands this and his persistence of incorporating Tuk in his music has begun to pay dividends.

Poonka's performance of his songs has been heavily dependent on his arrangers who have concentrated on the use of harmony. Therefore most of the arrangements used to present Poonka's compositions in the first decade of his performances have played down the traditional Tuk rhythms. This is not to say that they have not made concessions to Poonka and utilized his own playing here and there in the music. Essentially, however, these arrangers have concentrated on calypso rhythms with Tuk as decoration in parts of the song, usually at the end or in a chorus break.

Poonka has worked with arrangers such as Smokey Roett, Derry Etkins, Ricky Brathwaite, Mike Sealy and Nicholas Brancker—all excellent arrangers and producers. However, it was Nicholas Brancker who was able to throw off the dominance of the harmonies in the arrangement and who not only incorporated more Tuk rhythms, but sustained those rhythms from the beginning to the end of the song. A good example of this is his production of Poonka's *Tuk in me Head* produced in 1992.

NICHOLAS BRANCKER

What he also did was capture the importance of the Bum Drum (the big Bass drum) as the defining pulse of the rhythm.

CHRIS ALLMAN

If one listens to the music from 1992 onwards, one will see the maturing of Tuk as Nicholas (with MADD, krosfyah, et al.) and Chris Allman and, to a lesser extent, John Roett and more recently Eric Lewis, begin to transfer different aspects of the traditional Tuk rhythms to other instruments.

Just one word on the dispute between Poonka and Eddy Grant: Grant may have incorporated some Tuk rhythms in his Ring Bang. But he has also incorporated Jab-Jab and other rhythms. Ring Bang is not Bumbatuk and Bumbatuk is not Ring Bang. Tuk and Ring Bang may coincide at certain points and nothing is wrong with that. Unfortunately, Grant has limited the use of Ring Bang by copyrighting the name which allows him to claim royalties from artists who use the name.

Poonka, as the voice of Bumbatuk, can be proud of his contribution to the modernization of Tuk.

My dream of having large Tuk bands—fifty Bum drums, fifty kitties, fifty flutes, assorted triangles and other percussion instruments—on the road on Kadooment day has been superceded by the electronic Tuk rhythms of today's music. Listen and you will hear.

Ahoy, de Landship Pon de Reef!

IT WAS 1863 and William Barclay, also know as Arthur, was nine years old when he mudda tell he they were going home. He had heard the stories from the time he was a little boy and he was looking forward to it.

As a matter of fact, Little Willie was glad when he mudda and grandmudda join de new group in Seaman's Village, in Britton's Hill, that used to dance to the Bum Drum and dress up pretty. He was looking forward to joining the Cornwall.

Willie never went pon a boat yet. The closest he come to one was a maypole that he used to paddle pon. He used to hear all de old men talk bout de schooners and all de different place dey went. But he did still frighten to get in the moses that was going to take him out of the careenage to the big boat in Carlisle Bay. All his dreams bout dressing up for the parade gone. It was replaced by a tingling expectation like if frays was nibbling at he toes.

There were 365 people that day in 1865 that left Barbados for Liberia on the *Brig Cora*.

And the parade that William wanted to be in still went ahead. And so the Barbados Landship Movement was born in the heart of Britton's Hill in a place known as Seaman's Village with the participants supposedly mocking English sailors.

Barbados was a forlorn place for African people. Slavery was supposed to be done, but the conditions and reality didn't change much and did not change for a hundred years after emancipation. Villages were cramped. Houses were roofed with cane trash.

Hard ground-dirt, the floor. Mattresses, if they existed, were made with kuss-kuss or sour grass.

Houses were for sleeping. They fanned out around compounds like African villages, which they were. Cooking was outdoors at the back, social gathering at the front, in the road, on the common ground.

Work began when light cracked the night and ended when night fall down. Sometimes the sun loitered to meet the moon, forcing duppies into trees where story-tellers bent wires to hook them out for nosy children.

Life was not nice. It was unrelentingly hard and unvaried. Static and routine. Only a few children escaped the confines of this plantation routine, finding innocent relief in the schools of the Church and its beliefs.

Into this life came the Landship with its uniforms, its regalia, its ranks and its dance. An organization with its meeting turns of savings, its common purpose of mutual assistance, of discipline, of respect and authority.

The Barbados Landship developed into a crucible of cultural expression, a repository of traditional dances combined to depict

BARBADOS LANDSHIP

the fortunes and misfortunes of mythical British naval vessels at sea. Most people were therefore only exposed to the public aspects of the Landship—the manoeuvres consisting of the dance routines ritualizing everything from the engine room to rough seas and man overboard.

But the Landship offered much more to a community bound by the vestiges of slavery. In the world of the village, a Landship Captain or Commander was tantamount to being a Village Chief. This community leadership role was recognized by the courts, which often assigned wayward boys to their care rather than impose a custodial sentence.

Membership in the Landship required discipline while offering prestige. Members learned cooperation and would travel all over the island to meet and socialize with other groups. The movement brought a cohesion to an otherwise amorphous set of communities.

There was such a sense of racial oneness that in the 1910s when Marcus Garvey and the Universal Negro Improvement Association (UNIA) was active, the nurses section of the

MARCUS GARVEY

Landship adopted the Black Star symbol of the Garvey Movement as its insignia. From then on they became known as Stars and wore Black Stars on their shoulders.

Bajans have had long practice in cutting and contriving in order to survive. To retain access to their traditional music, Africans had adopted the acceptable military drums and formed the Tuk Band. Traditional drums and other noisy instruments were banned early during slavery. Even now, Tuk Bands still start their performances with march rhythms or with a waltz to camouflage the complex African rhythms.

The Landship is a similar camouflage. Like many African secret societies, the Landship provided an opportunity to belong, to dress up and to perform. The combination of the Tuk Band and the dances linked to an organized structure was a total winner.

There is still much to be uncovered about the Landship. It is one of the few indigenous Caribbean institutions. It has survived since 1863 when it was founded by Moses Ward. This makes it

HUGH CUMMINS

older than any of the imported social organizations: Boy Scouts, Girl Guides, Lions, Rotary, Kiwanis, B & Ps, Jaycees, Optimists, et al.

Changing social conditions and the evolution and devolution of political power to blacks have affected the Landship Movement. In the 1930s, there were over a hundred ships with large membership. Premier Hugh Gordon Cummins and Sir Mencea Cox were founding members of the Landship Council. Today, there are only a few landships left.

MENCEA COX

It would be a disaster to allow the Landship to run aground and rust away. It is an institution that has sustained us in adversity, entertained us royally, and provided us with a continuity to our past.

We must save the Landship for future generations. Not necessarily in its present form, but save it we must. There is a body of knowledge of our traditional dances that must be secured.

The National Trust and the Museum have salvaged houses, equipment, furniture, documents and artifacts too numerous to mention. All important to our cultural heritage, but none as fragile and important as the Landship. By the way, William Arthur Barclay reached Liberia safely. He became President of Liberia from 1904 to 1912.

Dr. Aviston Downes, writing in *The Journal of the Barbados Museum and Historical Society* (Vol XLVIII: 2002), makes the point that:

AVISTON DOWNES

> There is a remarkable similarity between the Landship and the friendly societies established in Sierra Leone in the 19th Century by members of the Kru who migrated there from Liberia. For example, on March 1888 the Bar Pyne Poli was established in the Kru community in Chapel Street, Sierra Leone and by the early 1890s the First Class Settra Kroo Sardo Boh Pyne Poh Number Two White Uniform Society was established there. Members and officers dressed in naval uniforms and occupied positions such as Captain, Purser, Quarter Master, Bosun and Ship's Doctor. Lodge rooms were often outfitted like ships. Kru men were extensively employed in the British merchant navy as Frost's work demonstrates.

He concludes that "no doubt, seamen from the Caribbean like Moses Wood would have served with them." I have a different interpretation: the 365 Bajans including young Arthur Barclay would more likely have taken their practices with them and maintained them in the context of Liberia since the similarity is so complete. This would also give fillip to the theory on the origins of the Landship in the early 1860s.

Next week, a solution for the future.

The Landship: Mek It Live Forever!

THE BARBADOS Mutual Assurance Company is the oldest indigenous institution in Barbados. Founded in 1841, it was established to protect planters from the vicissitudes of the sugar industry and predatory hustlings of British merchants.

The Barbados Landship Movement was founded in 1863 and is the oldest indigenous social organization in Barbados. It was established to protect former slaves and their descendants from the vicissitudes of the sugar industry, particularly the perennial hard times. Like the Mutual, the Landship believed in the pooling of resources to provide assistance for its members during sickness and at death. However, it also provided members with a sense of well-being, a sense of community and a sense of dignity.

As we approach the beginning of the twenty-first century, we see the Mutual continuing to go from strength to strength, while the Landship is shrinking and steadily withering away.

CLYDE GOLLOP

Last week I raised the spectre of this tragedy, for that best describes what we are witnessing.

The Landship attracted people like Dr. Hugh Gordon Cummins, who became Premier of Barbados in the late 1950s; Sir Mencea Cox, member of the House Assembly and one of the first Ministers of the BLP government during the 1950s; Sir Clyde Gollop, one of Barbados' most outstanding Community Developers; and Mrs. Gertrude Eastmond, businesswoman and member of the House of Assembly.

GERTRUDE EASTMOND

No country can afford to lose patrimony with this type of legacy.

Last week, I spoke of the Landship running aground on a reef. It is time to salvage it and put it on the dry dock.

I am proposing that the Landship Movement be redesigned as a Youth Movement, to be installed in every school, primary and secondary, in the island.

Such an organization should have the following components:

- ☐ The structural composition of the Landship should be preserved adding additional ranks with badges and medals for achievement similar to Scouting and Guiding.

- ☐ Uniforms may vary according to the school. The school may use a wider combination of designs and colours, especially school colours.

- ☐ Traditional set sequences of dance movements should be maintained with provision for variations within these movements. This is to facilitate competition in the future.

- ☐ Fees must be charged for membership. These fees along with other contributions and receipts from fund-raising activities must be run by the members of the Landship headed by the Bursar of the Landship. Meeting turns (Susu) must be a part of the organization. An advisor from the school staff or banking institution would assist.

- ☐ Traditional music (Tuk drumming, flute playing and

percussion) must also be taught as an adjunct of the Landship.

☐ A Landship should carry the name of the school.

☐ A Patron should be appointed for the organization.

☐ There should be four categories for the Landship organizations: Moses, Seines, Lighters and Schooners.

A permanent secretariat would be required to oversee the development and maintenance of this new Landship organization. A staff of three persons attached to the NCF would man this secretariat and be responsible for teaching the dance, music and organizational aspects of the Landship.

I believe that government should appoint as soon as possible a non-partisan committee to plan and develop this concept to its fullest. In addition to representation of political parties, the following should be represented: the Landship Movement, the Defence Force, the Ministries of Education, Culture and Youth Affairs, the Association of Bankers, the BSTU, the BUT, the Secondary and Primary Head Teachers Associations, the NCF, the Ministry of Culture, the Community Development Department, and the Mutual.

Finally, I would like to suggest that a pilot project of twelve schools be implemented in 1998, three in each category, that is, Moses, Seines, Lighters and Schooners.

National development is not just about buildings and roads and airports and harbours. It is not just about language and maths and what was and when. It is not about aping and mocking others and fashioning oneself in someone else's image.

National development is about us, about our own physical and spiritual well-being. Modern culture values documentation and records of achievement. Common folk are seldom documented. Occasionally, a song may extol the virtues of a community hero. It is remembered from time to time. By and large, however, these nameless and forgotten ancestors of ours are condemned to be forgotten.

The Landship sustained many a battered spirit and comforted many souls when there was nothing else. To survive one hundred and thirty-four years from its origins in 1863 with little help from governments or successful financial institutions is testimony of its strength and importance. Only some churches and parliament can claim such longevity.

My plea goes out to all Bajans: please, do not let the Landship die. Maybe you don't like my suggestion and you have a better one. I don't care. Put it forward. But let us save the pearls of our past.

Mr. Prime Minister, you are from Mile-and-a-Quarter. I am sure you were aware as a boy the importance of the Landship over in Rose Hill and the Tuk Band in Benhill (or is it Benn Hill?). Your recent forays of defining a role for Barbados in the Americas can only be sustained by a people who are stoutly sure of themselves.

The Barbados Landship Movement has served us well. Let us carry it into the future with assurance and dignity.

Mek it live forever!

The Search for Lindy Bradshaw

MY OLE man used to talk about him all the time. No one, he said, could play a guitar like Lindy Bradshaw. He said that Lindy Bradshaw could play any tune, backwards, forwards and sideways if necessary. Hum it and he would play it before yuh finish the first line.

After studying overseas, I returned to search for Lindy Bradshaw. I know that if he living he gine be old, but I did want to hear he play real bad. I travelled with a tape recorder hoping I would find he and record he playing a few tunes. And so the search started.

First I went to Eva Archer's shop in Baxter's Road opposite Chapman Street. It later became Enid's bar, a hangout for Richard Pryor and other Hollywood notables. Everybody did know Eva. She had nuff politician friends and she used to serve the sweetest black pudden and souse after my Aunt Sybil who lived in Speightstown.

Eva promised me that if she see he she would call me. Weeks pass and I ent hear nutten from she so I pass by she again. She tell me try Big Red Best John Bull Bar next to Harrison's furniture workshop, right where de stationary now is down in Milk Market, behind Harrison's No. 1 duty free store. Red Best say he ent suh he fuh weeks and to try over by Darnley Greenidge place Independence Inn.

Independence Inn was pon de top floor in de upstairs building next to de barbershop at de corner of Fairchild Street where de

National Insurance Building now is. I went upstairs looking fuh Darnley Greenidge, but he din dey. But ah meet one of dem St. Lucian gal dat he went and buy from dey mudda like goat. Duh used to call dis one Doo Doo, she was a lil fine ting, bout sixteen wid curly curly hair dat she used to brush back from she forehead.

Is she who tell me how Darnley Greenidge buy she and tell she four fuh he and one fuh she and she din kno whuh he did talking bout. And how she shut she self up in a room and nuff nuff water come out she eye dat she cudda fill up a calabash and bathe in it. A nex woman explain to she dat she was to charge de men five dollars, tek one fuh sheself and gi Darnley Greenidge four. After dat she was my fren and used to tell me who sleeping wid who at each hotel cause wen de hotel workers come to pick a fare, dem used to tell she whuh used to go on at de Hilton and ting. So I nevah did find Lindy Bradshaw, but she promise to ask bout he and lemme know.

Ah pass through Suttle Street several nights, and during de day too. Ah ask Sunna Murrell. Sometimes ah had to go in de back whey dem does gamble and ask he if he had any news fuh me. But he neva see Lindy Bradshaw fuh months. He tell me to guh nex door at de Tradewinds and ask Sam Gibbs. Same story— Sam ent see he neither.

Nex ah try Nelson Street, up and down, from Stanley Goddard place, Zanzibar to Gwen Workman shop. Not a soul ent see he. I went round de corner by Mitchie Stanford rum shop, I tink it was call de Palm Bar or something so, dey so by Rediffusion. Not a man ent see he and fuh dat ah had to stand muh hand and buy a round.

A nex' Sarduh I went round by Palmetto Square, out by de Olympic Theatre to see if anybody out dey cud tell me whey Lindy Bradshaw live. By now it looking as if he dead and I did feelin real bad causing I did wan to hear dis man real real bad.

And right out dey in the road whey de men did drinking I see Shilling. I ent kno why I ent look fuh Shilling an ask he eva since. And Shilling tell me dat Lindy Bradshaw sick an was at some family of his up in St. Patricks, Christ Church. But he too ent see he fuh weeks so he din kno if he was still sick or dead or alright.

Dat Sunday, I pack my tape recorder in de Spitfire and wid Mudda Africa in tow, we head out to St. Patricks. Mudda Africa is anudder story fuh a nex' time. Wen I reach St. Patricks dis Sunday afternoon, de whole place shut down tight tight tight. You kno how um is wid Bajans pon a Sunday. So at first I was a lil bit doubtful, but since I was determine to find Lindy Bradshaw, ah decide to knock pun ev'ry door if ah had to. An ah had to. But nuh body en know he.

Just when ah was about to give up, ah look down de line behind a wall house and ketch a door ajar. De kuss-kuss grass did blocking muh view, but de door look like a shop door. Dis was de fust shop that had someting gine on so ah drive down de line dodging de linemark stakes sticking up in de track.

Ah knock pon de door and somebody shout "come round by de window!" Ah went round dey and ask dem if dem know Lindy Bradshaw and whey I cud fine he. Dem tell me guh back to de door. Wen de door open, sitting pon a bench in de corner was a wizen little black man hunched over a guitar under he right armpit. He said to me, "Ise Lindy Bradshaw. Who you?"

With that I recorded Lindy Bradshaw for three hours. He played four part harmony finger-picking style, but unfortunately time had taken its toll and his fingers were a little slow in finding the frets.

More unfortunately, ah nex Mudda Africa tek de tapes an trow dem in de sea.

Sweet Sweet Music and Memories

I AM privileged to have been a member of St. Mary's Anglican Church choir with the likes of Lion Man, Blair Murray, Ormond Scott, Rudolph Hinds, Charles Hinds and organist Bentley Callender.

Blair Murray was a table tennis champion. He was short and small with a voice as delicate as that of the little yellow breast cane bird.

Lion Man was tall and lanky and had a stride that was doubled by the size of his foot. His was the voice of a blackbird, strong, powerful and black to the core.

Rudolph Hinds was a baritone whose operatic sounds marinated in the marrow of his bones and resonated Paul Robeson's majesty in its definition.

RUDOLPH HINDS

Ormond Scott, a tailor by profession, was a weaver of spells like a vodoun high priest. His tenor voice, sensuous and sweet in its intensity, conjured images of an African wanderer, wutless yet fragile. He was also a member of the ruff-necked Chapman Lane Village Choir.

Charles Hinds was also a tailor. He was a gentle, polite man. He was a composer who captured in his anthems the extravagance of his dreams and feelings, European in its form, African in

BENTLEY CALLENDER

its feeling. The Eagle Hall Village Choir which he founded and directed expressed his ideas and thoughts in a singular voice.

Bentley Callender, a professional librarian, was an elegant man, certainly not a nerd, whose only standard in music was the European masters. But as devout as he was to this Euro-classical tradition, he would open the door for those (Charles Hinds, Ramsay) like himself who tried to capture it with their compositions.

With the exception of Bentley Callender, these men were the primary soloists in St. Mary's Choir.

My membership in St. Mary's Choir also exposed me to the brethren who came to hear the singing and the sermon, but who remained outside huddled at the windows. These men made up what I thought was the real choir. I looked forward to Papa Motts driving slowly behind them, listening to them as they wended their way up Broad Street, across the front of the Fountain in Trafalgar Square by the bus stand, across the Swing Bridge and up Bay Street.

No organ accompaniment. No other instruments. Just voices in sweet harmony, voices laced with green rum from three-gill bottles.

These inspired, ad hoc choirs chanted hymns, ancient and modern, and made them sound as if they were sung by a thousand voices instead of ten or twelve. The feelings of divinity, of devoutness, were unmistakable. I never heard or felt that emotion in St. Mary's choir or any other choir. The closest to it was round River Road mouth, in the little island garden, where a Brother Smith used to line-out the words for his transient congregation.

Later I was to hear it in the Pentecostal churches in Tudor Bridge, especially after Janet (1955) when the churches were filled with those who had to seek shelter. And then in the sixties in Merricks, St. Phillip, and in the new bus-stand on Fairchild Street by Granville Williams and his Tie-Heads. And from the Shango and Santeria recordings from Trinidad and Cuba respectively.

Except for Tuk Bands, these voices are my most stringent reminders of Christmas. There were not only heard at Christmas, of course, but for some reason I always associate them with Christmas and recall them. As a result I have these very powerful images, images of sounds, that echo and resonate now in my memory.

I can recall the five o'clock Christmas foreday-morning services, the splendour of Queen's Park with the Police Band of Captain Raison, and the pompassetters strutting like marathon runners from the Governor's Gate to Nelson Gate, back and forth, showing off their new clothes. The only things that were prettier were kites at Easter.

I close my eyes and smell the smell of the rare English apples, the peppermint of comfort, and the pan-boilers' delight, sugar-cakes. But none of these can capture the power and essence of what I heard then and still hear now in the crevices of my mind.

The Hungry Man from Hillaby

IT WAS either 1956 or 1957. It was either the second or third Annual Conference of the Democratic Labour Party (DLP). Forbes Burnham was the guest speaker. It was held in Queen's Park at Queen's Park House. Upstairs. This was before it was the Daphne Hackett Theatre and before it was the Queen's Park Theatre and before it was the Civic Theatre. It was an open space like downstairs with a shallow (in height, width and depth) stage at one end.

The conference itself was well attended, but I cannot recall any of its contents except that Burnham was one hell of a good speaker. What I do remember, however, was lunchtime.

J.E.T. BRANCKER

Theodore Brancker and Cameron Tudor were the two representatives for St. Lucy. Those were the days of double member constituencies. Brancker was a long-standing member while Tudor was a more recent electee whose election Owen T. Allder claimed was his doing with the help of Tudor's father, James A. Tudor, a well-known shopkeeper and Garveyite.

Both Brancker and Tudor were known to attend every wedding, christening, wake and Service-o-song in St. Lucy. So you could say they were well known to their constituents. And although

CAMERON TUDOR

I was not a St. Lucy constituent, I too knew these two members of parliament from St. Lucy.

That Sunday afternoon, under the spread-out Banyan tree between the Steel Shed and the Queen's Park restaurant, used then as a soup kitchen by the Bridgetown City Council, some St. Lucy supporters of the two members of parliament laid out a feast on an oil cloth that was unbelievable.

First, there was a small wash-pan of peas and rice with pig tail sticking out all over the place; a leg of pork with a crispy skin that sounded like a gun shot when it was bitten; a leg ham planted with clove like a garden or the head of a kinky hair little boy; at least six baked chickens with stuffing oozing out the neck hole at one end and the belly covering the pope's nose at the other; beef stew—cassareeped, dark and mysterious; and some type of goat.

Supporting this symphony of taste were roasted sweet potatoes, yellow and white still in their jackets, burnt black and ashened, waiting to be peeled; yam; pumpkin; lettuce; watercress; and beets looking like oversized exotic purple coins.

To wash this down, there was a large mauby can sweating in the noon time heat, offering whiffs of aromatic vanilla and another wash-pan of Oranjeboon, the Dutch beer that was the passion of Branks, on a large block of ice.

This feast was for the two representatives from St. Lucy and their guests. There were few guests. Little was left. Their prodigious appetites were legendary. So too was Cammie's brother, Martin, who was known to snack on a dozen eggs before breakfast and to carry a dozen salt breads in one pocket and a couple dozen fish cakes in the other in case he got hungry.

Thinking about this reminds me of a song that was popular in Barbados at the time about the legendary Hungry Man from Hillaby.

Chorus
Man is known round de town
He is known as a good food hound
Eat in the road and eat in the street
Is de hungry man from Hillaby.

Verse 1
 Jump high in de air
Sight Zephirin store down dey
Before de man could hit de ground
He had all o' Zephirin store yam down.

Verse 2
Went one day to the gates of hell
De devil say young man yuh doing well
Grab de devil and trow he down
And yam off all the devil night gown

There were many more verses. Lord Radio recorded a version of it. Last I heard, the original composer was a watchman at Shamrock in Baxter's Road.

Sometimes legends are real. Think about all them other legends wunna hear bout.

Dear Eddy Grant

WHEN DENNIS Bovell confided in
me years ago that he had helped to
persuade you to move to Barbados,
I was more than elated. I had no idea
how we as Bajans would benefit, but I
thought that your presence here could
make a difference. And it did.

DENNIS BOVELL

You established your home, your
recording studios and your recording company at Bailey's
Plantation, St. Philip and bought and rebuilt Caribbean
Pepperpot in St. Lawrence, Christ Church.

You adopted a coterie of artists headed by Gabby and Grynner,
hired a number of young Bajan musicians to work with you in
your studio as well as on the road. The exposure given to these
young artists have in my mind triggered the development
of today's musical successes. Some will disagree with this
assessment, but as they used to say about Errol Barrow, all roads
lead back to Eddy Grant.

Over the years, most of these artists have absorbed your
production techniques, built on them, and have produced a
body of commercial/party music that has impacted heavily
on the Caribbean over the last ten years. And overall, there is
also a sophistication that has evolved, a sophistication about
presentation, performance and the business of music.

I am not suggesting you are responsible for all of these things, as other influences are also important. But you came right after the most significant exposure that Bajan artists have ever had, and that was CARIFESTA in 1981.

In the interim, you have almost single-handedly forced Caribbean people into a consciousness about their musical heritage with your retrieving of old calypsos and calypsonians, particularly the works of the Roaring Lion, Spoiler, Sparrow, Kitchener and Terror. I also know of your personal commitment to and support of the family of one of the most important Jamaican producers.

But you have also given Bajan artists a sense and understanding of the music business. You can see this in the number of music publishing companies that have developed in recent years. As a matter of fact, I never tire of repeating a story you told me. I don't know if you remember it.

But as the story goes, you were stopped on the street in London by a young West Indian brother who was apparently broke and wanted to sell you a song that he wrote. He wanted some ridiculous sum like fifty pounds. You persuaded him to come to your office where you lent him the money. You then gave him a lecture about selling his music and convinced him to keep the song.

It turned out that one of the top groups (UB40?) recorded the song and it became a major international hit. The young man was now living like a prince, new house and fancy cars, based on the royalties he received for that song.

You too have indicated the importance of how you own and control your own music. And as a matter of fact, that ownership is responsible for your own successes. And then, your business partners tried to steal your music and your businesses. This betrayal has undermined all the personal work that you have been doing over the last two or three years by distracting you.

Many of the artists that worked with you have gone on to work with others. All except one man, who has remained loyal to you in the extreme, and that is Gabby—Anthony Carter.

You have said that Gabby is the greatest talent you know. You have guided his career for the last fifteen years. You have taught him the intricacies of being a good performer and writer—from diction in singing to universality of content in composing.

And Gabby responded. *Hit It, Cassandra, Debra,* and so on.

But Gabby has also demonstrated that he is the King and only time and reflection can truly assess his composing and performances. When you look back at his work, most of it is brilliant. And there are those songs that he has given to others that he himself cannot even recall.

But as a King, his recorded work is too little, too few, too unreflecting of his brilliance. And there are many people who would like to produce music for Gabby so as to satisfy his subjects, particularly since you are unavailable (distracted!). Gabby says they will have to ask you.

And what do you say? That you have no written contract with Gabby and he is free to do what he wants. But you know that Gabby won't do that. He is loyal to you to the core. He believes

JIMMY CLIFF, GABBY AND EDDY GRANT

251

in you and will not go against you for anything. Of all the artists who have worked with you, Gabby has unrepentantly remained an Eddy Grant loyalist.

I am sure you cannot say that about any other artist.

This open letter to you is a plea for you to give Gabby the 'OK' to record with other producers. These producers know how tough a businessman you are and how adroit and particular you are about copyright. They fear litigation and whatever else.

In the meantime, Gabby suffers. Gabby's subjects suffer. You suffer since you control all of Gabby's publishing. There is no music flowing and Gabby is overflowing with music.

Many of us have approached you privately about getting Gabby's music out there. He needs it to fuel his live performances. Only you, Eddy, can give the go ahead. Tell him! Release him from his bond of loyalty.

The Caribbean Music Awards

THE CARIBBEAN is best known worldwide for three things: tourism, sports, and music.

By the Caribbean, I mean from Belize to Barbados, from the Bahamas to the Guianas (Guyana, Suriname and Cayenne) and all the islands in between. Some are best known for their beaches, others for their natural and man-made heritage.

By Sports, I mean cricket, athletics, soccer, baseball, boxing, water sports, and all the other sports that we have international ratings in. Our sporting successes are often centred around individual performances. Cricket is the only team sports with a clear regional identity that does both.

By Music, I mean Mambo, Salsa and Merengue of the Spanish-speaking islands; Compas, Zouk and Beguine of the French-speaking islands; and Reggae, Soca and Calypso of the English-speaking islands. This is not an exhaustive list of all the popular forms of music in the Caribbean, but one that will give you an idea of what there is. And of course the carnivals and like festivals that are the major vehicles for this music.

Having defined my terms, let me state my premise. *I believe that the government and the people of Barbados should invest deeply in the music industry and the company producing the Caribbean Music Awards.*

There are several reasons for this suggestion: Caribbean Music in all its forms and Caribbean musical artists are the best-known Caribbean personalities worldwide.

The Caribbean Music Awards (CMA) is a young show in its sixth year and can only grow into a major international event to reflect the interest and spread of the music.

Such an investment will be conditional on Barbados becoming the permanent Caribbean Home of the CMA.

This year the CMA came after the Congaline Festival, but from next year it should come before so that all the participating groups can participate in Congaline, thus converting Congaline into the most important Caribbean Music Festival, providing the Barbados Tourism Authority with a major international event to market.

Music has the makings of a major industry. For people who believe in steel mills and fossil fuel industries, there is a tendency to dismiss the power, influence and diffusion of music. In the 1960s, the Beetles helped to shore up the British government's international reserves.

Caribbean music is now ubiquitous throughout the world. We tend to forget that Calypso made a tremendous impact on the USA in the 1930s. Trinidadian artists like Lion, Atilla and Executor established Calypso in the USA. As early as the 1910s, the Barbadian-born Trinidadian Lionel Belasco established a formidable recording career with Victor Records. It was Harry Belafonte in the 1950s that finally gave Calypso a high international profile.

Afro-Cuban and Afro-Brazilian music made its way into the movies and popular music in the USA and the world. By the 1950s, Mambo and Cha-Cha were topping the charts in various disguises. The Rumba of Cuba seasoned the ancestral rhythms of the Congo which in turn was to spread all over Africa.

The phenomenal impact of Bob Marley was to take Jamaican and Caribbean music further than any of us could imagine, across every continent irrespective of language and race. Reggae more than any other music and the image of the dreadlocks Rasta is almost sacrosanct in every hamlet, every village throughout the world.

The Caribbean Diaspora in the USA and Canada, UK and Europe has established markets for Soca and Zouk and other Caribbean musics. Witness the number of Carnivals in the USA and Canada. In the UK, Notting Hill is the biggest example of some thirty odd carnivals in the British Isles. In France, Belgium, Holland, Scandinavia and Germany, there are also Carnivals fueled by the music of the French and Dutch Islands.

In every nook and cranny, you will find Caribbean artists performing and spreading the gospel of Caribbean music. The music itself has its own converts and disciples doing the same.

The Caribbean Music Awards is obviously a show that recognizes the important of this music and is attempting to establish a way to reward the region and its artists in a collective way. I believe that the continuing growth of the Caribbean Music Awards is going to depend on the ability of the show's producers to remain in business long enough. Unfortunately, we in the Caribbean are not organized enough even to give the sort of support necessary to make the voting system effective. Actual play lists and record sales, playing of records from non-English speaking regions, contribute to the slow progress of the CMA surveys.

By investing in the CMA, Barbados stands to establish a pre-eminent position for itself and its music and its image as the Caribbean Music Centre of the world. Television bridges continents and all the other hurdles that slowed the progress of Caribbean Music.

There is a market out there, as I have indicated. Should we not be a part of the access to that market? I am sure the Tourism Authority would see the residual benefits to Barbados by getting access to such a show on an annual basis.

Caribbean artists have already established names for themselves throughout the world. CMA will give recognition to those artists. The same audience certainly will be interested in seeing how their favourite Caribbean artist will do. Are we not interested in the Emmys and the Oscar winners? And aren't these translated into revenues for the artists? I have no doubt that the same will be true for the recipients of the CMA Awards by the end of the decade.

This year the CMA took place after the Congaline Festival. I believe that it should take place at the same time as the Congaline Festival so that all the artists are available for Congaline. This will now enhance the power of Congaline as an event that can be marketed distinctly and separately from Crop Over. It would mean that Congaline can be completely internationalized, making it the appropriate vehicle for the CMA.

This is one of the directions in investment that the National Cultural Foundation should be encouraged to take on behalf of the government. Long-term planning is essential for the future of Barbados as a tourism destination, as well as for the development of its music industry and the myriad jobs that will develop as a result of this type of thinking and planning.

I also believe that an adjunct to this outreach in music should be the expansion of the Caribbean Broadcasting Union (CBU) which should invest in two or three broadcast stations in the USA for purposes of giving us access to our Caribbean diaspora and the other markets in the USA, Canada and Latin America. The rest will follow in due course.

Let Me Hear the Feet!

Let Me hear the Feet!

"Let me hear the Feet!"

Freddie Keppard, Jazz Trumpeter, 1907

AS THE twentieth century closes, we can say without contradiction that Africa and its people, wherever they were scattered, however they were treated, whatever they did, have succeeded in dominating the world with variations of its music.

This music, steeped in the rhythms of a continent that was described with prejudice as the Dark Continent, a continent of mystery and primitivism, has penetrated every barrier and reached the various people of the world and their cultures. It is a music that has been copied and imitated, but never created except by its originators.

Black Music, as the music of Africa and its Diaspora is often called, is difficult to define. There are so many variations coming from so many places, each presenting a different facet of a jewel that a hundred years ago was considered inferior and subordinate to that of other cultures, particularly European cultures.

There are four elements to Black Music. They are: rhythm, melody, lyrics and performance. The context in which these elements are presented may vary and can influence the content and emphasis on individual elements.

Rhythm cannot exist by itself. It is propelled by an assortment of percussion instruments that can be shaken, beaten, plucked or blown. Rhythm can be simple or complex or be made up of layers of simple tones. The combination of tones forms a melody. If listened to carefully, you can hear cycles of rhythm as simple repetitive melodies played on the percussion instruments.

One of the misconceptions about traditional African music is that it is static. It was never static then or now. The music is always absorbing new things and utilizing new technologies, while expressing an underlying continuity between the past and the present.

For example, there is no difference between the rhythms of Jamaican dancehall and traditional African music recorded, for example, in the 1920s by the Roosevelt expedition. The type of instrument may be different, but the use of the rhythms are the same. Similarly with James Brown or Edwin Yearwood or David Rudder.

African people have always been users of technology and used it to recreate the memories from the past regardless of the context in which they found themselves. When the great Cuban drummer Potato developed the tuned Conga drums in the 1950s, drummers all over adopted them and used them; the reason— simplicity. Normally untuned drums had to be heated in the sun or near a fire to get rid of the moisture from the drum head (goat skin, or whatever animal skin was being used.) The correct tone had to be achieved.

The ironsmith traditionally made gongs and other metal instruments. The steelband men used an industrial brake hub if it had the right tone. When King Oliver, Freddie Keppard, Buddy Bolden and Louis Armstrong made the trumpet leap through the silence of the night in Congo Square in New Orleans at the beginning of 20th Century, they were approaching the instrument with the same flair and virtuosity as Hausa trumpeters at the annual Sallah Festival in Northern Nigeria. Modernization and

FREDDIE KEPPARD

BUDDY BOLDEN

technology has not altered the continuum of African music.

Melody can exist without rhythm even though that rhythm can be simple and uncomplicated. It can consist of parallel melodic lines to form harmony. It can also be sequential with a call and a response. And it can be a combination of all of these things. Again dancehall chanting or soca call and response for action is nothing new, but more of the same tradition performed in a new context.

KING OLIVER

LOUIS ARMSTRONG

Lyrics can praise or condemn or be inane. Relevant or irrelevant. They can stand alone as poems, as literature, with little regard for rhythm or melody. Although they can give meaning to a song, understanding the lyrics is not a prerequisite to the enjoyment of a song. Linked to performance, the human voice is but another instrument, as can be found in today's soca/dancehall/rapping performers.

Because there was no differentiation between religious and secular life in Africa of the past, music performed a very important role in the life of African people. Therefore music was used at birth, at naming ceremonies, at weddings, at burial ceremonies, at work (particularly communal work), at worship, at play, for sporting activity, and for festivals.

Today the music is no different and without the lyrics, the same rhythms and melodies are used inside and outside of the church. And more importantly, there is no difference in terms of religious or secular dancing.

Today Trinidad and Tobago celebrates its Carnival. Last year David Rudder eloquently paid tribute to both Christianity (an adopted religion) and Shango in his High Mas and The Banana Death Song respectively. Anyone seeing his performance and his Shango moves would have seen a High Priest in action.

This dance, this movement on the streets, propelled and driven by rhythm sections known as engine rooms, with or without meaningful lyrics or strong melodies, is performance-driven by performer and participant alike.

When Freddie Keppard admonished his band in 1907 "Let me hear the feet," he was setting in motion the power of Black Music to make people dance. Like it or not, it is music for the feet and the music of the twentieth century.

No Heaven, no Earth, no America

IT WAS as if it was made for the small timber houses in Barbados, the ones called chattel houses that you could move like a horse or cow and carry from spot to spot. It had a trapezoid shape with the top wider than the bottom that allowed it to fit in a corner at just about head height, causing it to look down to the floor. It was suspended from a nail by a brass chain, and like a shookster, used the house as a resonating chamber.

Nearly everybody who had one hanging in their house had it in the front house near the window. It was nearly always stained brown like a piece of furniture, with the company's name in bold gold letters or some other contrasting colour across the top. Below the big eight-inch hole in the middle was a black knob that had two functions—on or off and loudness control.

It was a Rediffusion speaker that was known as Radio Distribution in the mid-forties before it was bought out by the British multinational company.

LOUIS JORDAN

It was from this speaker that I first heard the black classical music of jazz performed by some of the great masters: Louis Armstrong, Duke Ellington, Count Basie, Louis Jordan and many more. But it was the Duke and the Count that caught my attention as a little boy, compelling me to keep a log in a little blue note book

COUNT BASIE

LOUIS ARMSTRONG

on the number of times I heard their classic songs *Take the A Train* and *One O'Clock Jump.*

I soon graduated from this box that echoed through the community on early evenings with an invisible wall of sound when the request time and birthday greetings program called the names of friends and family across the island. Every box was on at full volume as people listened for their names or those of friends while looking out the window watching the children play.

I graduated to the Phillips table radio where I heard the voices of Michael Laing and Sam Ghany and Bob Gittens and later on Frank Pardo before he came to Barbados emanating from Radio Trinidad. I revelled in the Sunday afternoon gambits of Auntie Kay and her young talents.

But most of all I relished the Voice of America broadcast of *Music USA* and *Jazz USA.* The host of *Jazz USA* was Willis Conover who used Duke Ellington's *Take the*

DUKE ELLINGTON

A-Train as his theme. This version featured a vocal performance by the singer Betty Roche, who blew a vocal solo that gave me funny feelings, feelings I later was to discover had its parallels in orgasms.

And then in the latter part of the fifties, 1956 or '57, at fourten on Sunday afternoons, I heard the voice that a CNN reporter once called "the voice of god." Desmond Bourne. His was one of the literate alliterations encompassing not only the history of jazz performance, but included the gritty and fascinating stories of the performers.

It was Desmond Bourne, the voice of god, that introduced me to Duke's *A Drum is a Woman*, Duke's excursions about Madame Zajj (jazz backwards) who was born in

DESMOND BOURNE

the Caribbean, and her promiscuous travels to Congo Square in New Orleans, to Harlem in New York, and to the moon, cavorting in each place with the mysterious Caribbean Joe.

By 1958, I was a student in Canada. In 1959, I spent my summer vacation in New York listening to all these legends. I was surprised to find that many of these formidable performers were alive and well.

Lewisohm Stadium is the football stadium of Columbia University. In that summer of '59, it was the venue of my first jazz concert: Herbie Mann, Miles Davis and Duke Ellington. I paid fifty cents to see that concert and sat in the bleachers opposite the stage shell about a hundred and fifty metres away. I was well advised to take along a pair of binoculars and I am glad I did. It was an afternoon that I have never forgotten, hearing the Duke for the first time live with his fabulous band. I was impressed.

The last time I saw Duke was in a church. In the intervening years, I saw him in Central Park, at the street concerts in Harlem, at Forest Hills Tennis Stadium and numerous other shows. I had started collecting his music and books about him. The concert was held at the first A. M. E. Zion Church at Tompkins Avenue and McDonough Street in Brooklyn, New York, on March 10, 1966. It was the last time I saw him perform and it was different.

It was different because it was a Concert of Sacred Music, but it was uncompromising jazz that was solemn and respectful, raucous and sensual, happy and celebratory. Most of all it was exultant. It featured music from *Black, Brown and Beige, My People*, and *New World A' Coming*.

It featured the alto of Johnny Hodges, the baritone sax of Harry Carney, the clarinet of Jimmy Hamilton, the tenor sax of Paul Gonsalves, the trombone of Lawrence Brown, the trumpet of Cat Anderson, the drums of Louie Bellson, the violin and tap dancing of Ray Nance, the voices of Brock Peters, Esther Marrow, Eloise Owens and the combined choirs of the First A. M. E. Zion Church and the Garden State Choirs and of course the piano of Duke Ellington.

As Duke said in his introduction of *In the beginning God...*, "there was no heaven, no earth, no cabbage greens, no headache, no aspirin."

Without Duke Ellington, there is no twentieth century America.

Duke Ellington: Beyond Category

BOOKER T. Washington, the founder of the famous Tuskegee Institute in the USA, wrote in his biography *Up From Slavery* about how he visited the home of freed blacks in the 1890s and noticed that they owned an organ but no utensils for eating. No knife and fork. No spoon.

The family seemed very comfortable with their tradition, the African tradition, of eating communal meals from bowls with their fingers. But it was also clear to me that they possessed a very strong love for music and hence the expensive investment in the organ, technically speaking, a new instrument to them.

This love of music was all-encompassing and was a major part of the life of African-Americans during slavery and in the twenty or so years after slavery was abolished. The Fisk Jubilee Singers made their first tour in 1871 and soon America and Europe were raving about this 'new music' of Black Americans. The music was called Spirituals.

In 1897, Tom Turpin was the first black man to publish a ragtime song, *Harlem Rag* and in 1899, the soon to be legendary Scott Joplin published *Maple Leaf Rag*. Black Music was beginning to make its presence felt.

This did not stop racist

SCOTT JOPLIN

attitudes from taking away the freedom of African-Americans given to them by the Emancipation Proclamation. By 1891 Jim Crow (racist) legislation was enacted in a number of states to separate blacks from whites. Racism was considered 'scientific' and justifiable and dominated the attitudes of both State and Federal governments. The lynching of African-Americans was so commonplace that W. E. B. duBois and friends established the National Association for the Advancement of Coloured People (NAACP) in 1908 and later Marcus Garvey formed the United Negro Improvement Association (UNIA) in the 1910s.

It was in this context that Edward Kennedy Ellington was born in Washington, DC on April 29, 1899. Unlike the family described by Booker T. Washington, Ellington was given an aristocratic upbringing. His father was a part-time butler at the White House and his mother was a prim and proper housewife with high moral standards. Both of them played piano and young Ellington was sent to lessons from early. He was given the name Duke to reflect his fastidious appearance and his sweet mout.

DUKE ELLINGTON

This month we celebrate the centenary of Duke Ellington's birth. As a composer, musician, arranger, orchestrator and band leader, he has no peers. In spite of a viperous nest of racism, Duke Ellington has been able to rise above all and sundry to become one of the most formidable musicians of the twentieth century.

This is his legacy: over 50 years of leading and maintaining a full-time band; hiring over 800 musicians during this period in his bands, some staying as long as 35 years; producing over

2,000 compositions, over 10,000 recordings and over 20,000 performances while logging 10 million miles.

But Duke's legacy is far more than stats. He was a painter of moods, of feelings, of the lives of a people at work, at play, in pain and under stress. Duke Ellington, more than any other composer/ musician captured the culture of a people in a myriad of song portraits. He honed the sounds of surprise by harnessing the individual creativity of his band members. There is an optimism about these portraits. They are like rose buds of hope waiting to burst forth in a glory of colour from the sound of a horn, an agitated expectancy like the growls and swoops from the brass- fire of a Arthur Whetsol or a Bubber Miley or a Cootie Williams or a Ray Nance or a Cat Anderson or a chortling Clark Terry.

Or he may layer a petal with the dewy breath of a Johnny Hodges or a Ben Webster and provide a cushion for Harry Carney to bridge its fall. And sometimes he displays hues from seas and skies for Barney Bigard or Sidney Bechet to extract indigo dyes.

Or he may capture the hustle from *East St. Louis* to *Harlem at Daybreak* with the expressed rhythms of Sonny Greer or Sam Woodyard and the sanctified sermons of Tricky Sam Nanton's trombone.

But it was the tapestries that Duke weaved and rendered out of the total experiences and sufferings of the African-American in the twentieth century that charts him beyond category: *Black and Tan Fantasy; Black, Brown and Beige; A Tone Poem to Harlem; Liberian Suite; In the Beginning God; A Drum is a Woman; Deep South Suite; Shakespeare Suite; Jump for Joy; Anatomy of a Murder; Virgin Island Suite; La Plus Belle Africaine; New Orleans Suite; Afro-Eurasian Eclipse;* etc.

When you take a retrospective look at Duke Ellington's music, you cannot help but notice that he was responding continuously to what was happening around him and the presence of the different persons performing in his band. Each decade produced a different sound for the band while at the same time retaining that distinctive Duke Ellington signature.

Duke Ellington, a giant of the twentieth century.

Bob Marley, the 20th Century Greatest West Indian

"...Every song is a classic, from the messages of love to the anthems of revolution - the album is a political and cultural nexus drawing inspiration from the Third World and then giving voice to it the world over."

TIME, declaring the Bob Marley and the Wailers Album, EXODUS, as the best music album of the century.

I HAD just moved to Jamaica and was making the expected rounds attending a number of parties, being introduced to and meeting people. I was impressed by the friendliness and the openness of everyone. As I wandered into this particular group, I overheard the end of a conversation: "...the two worst things that happen to Jamaica was Marcus Garvey and Bob Marley." I was shocked. I asked for clarification and it was repeated to me just as I said, except the tone was a lot more acerbic.

MARCUS GARVEY

I said to myself, *but these people like them mad*, and was about to launch into a defense of Garvey and Marley when my wife took my elbow and said it was time to go.

I remember that incident well and at first it was a conundrum to

BOB MARLEY

271

me. Why would black people consider Garvey and Marley as worse than Gilbert, the hurricane?

Garvey was a man who articulated the dreams of African people to be free; to be returned to Africa if that was the only place that they could be free. He sought respect for black people the world over knowing how much they had suffered and were still suffering from being enslaved; from being maligned, castigated and deprecated.

His was not a new voice, but it was a powerful and articulate voice that was able to reach the greatest mass of black people at the start of the 20th Century. He created no miracles, he preached no violence. He encouraged people to put on their 'Sunday-go-to-meetings' or their uniforms/costumes and marched with him with dignity and pride. He gave them hope and a vision. Africa for Africans at home and abroad! He tried to build unity.

From the day the first African was captured and forced to come to the new world, he longed for the day that he could return. On the slave ships, they preferred to escape and jump overboard and die so that their souls could return home to Africa. The Martiniquan poet Aime Cesaire captured this feeling most eloquently in his poem *Cahier d'un retour au pays natal* (Return to My Native Land).

And what was Bob Marley's crime? To raise his voice in song, to sing songs of freedom to us, to ask us all to liberate our minds from mental slavery, to free ourselves from thoughts of inferiority and second class citizenship, to assert ourselves and our love. To reject violence. He asserted blackness and rejected the images of culturedness. His image of Rastafari was the antithesis of Afro-saxonism.

And then I realized that they, the party people, the Afro-saxonists, the children of Babylon, the aspirants to the mantle of the plantation four-poster bed, could not accept Garvey and his

Pan-Africanist tribes, nor could they accept a man who shook his nappy dreadlocks in their face and stole the minds of their children.

And to this day, they will not accept him as a national hero. Not enough of them are dead yet, as happened with Bajans and Clement Payne.

In Exodus he says:

Open your eyes and look within.
Are you satisfied with the life you're living?
We know where we are going
We know where we are from.
We're leaving Babylon
We're going to our father's land.
Exodus!
Movement of Jah people...

But Bob Marley was not just a messenger of rebelliousness to Jamaican youth (Trevor Marshall I will come back to this!), but to youth, irrespective of national origin and colour all over the world. Like Garvey, Marley reaches the dispossessed with his music, singling with their despair, giving them hope of a solution. He was like the Pied Piper of Hamlyn.

It is clear that youth have recognized him for what he was, is and forever will be.

And to top it off, the BBC named Bob Marley's *One Love*, the song of the 20th Century.

But wait a minute, what about the rest of us? Bob Marley is the best known West Indian in the world. He has made the image of the Rastaman respectable and acceptable worldwide. We are being told by the outside world that he was the greatest. How come we don't use the Rastaman image to promote tourism? ...I guess some more people have to dead.

One love!

The Beat goes on, or
Two for the Count

IT WAS a great year for Sparrow. 1969. *Sa Sa Ay, Sixty Million Frenchmen, The Lizard, Sparrow Dead, Who She Go Cry For, Cockfight, Pussy Cat*. Port-of-Spain was alive with Sparrow's songs fluttering on the hot humid winds from the hills of Laventile to the yards of St. James.

My first carnival in Trinidad. Pan yards. Despers. Invaders. Starlift. And Sco—Scofield Pilgrim.

Scofield Pilgrim, Bajan expatriate, teacher at Queen's Royal College (QRC), jazz lover, philosopher. My first encounters with Sco lead to an invitation to visit QRC where he conducted a jazz workshop with students and others who were interested in developing their skills in jazz.

Sco played a big mudda fiddle. Not very well, I thought at the time, and I haven't changed my mind since then. But he had an enthusiasm about jazz as a Caribbean art form that I had not heard before.

In his inimitable style, with mannerisms that suggested the nervousness of a ground dove, Sco explored the idea of the Caribbean jazz based on calypso. He talked about the early work of Rupert Clemendore... and the rhythms of pan... and the road march. Even though he could not as a performer implement these concepts, he articulated for me a new vision about the potential of our music.

He introduced me to a young architect by the name of Clive

Alexander, aka Zanda. Zanda was a member of the Gayap Workshop along with Sco and several other people. Zanda was a percussive player whose melodic lines echoed traditional calypso, while his rhythms reflected those of the road marches. Zanda's compositions and performances remain indelible landmarks in the development of Caribbean jazz.

Sco was a salesman of jazz and his mind remained in perpetual motion, selling the concept of jazz across the region to jazz musicians, jazz fans and any other folk who would listen. He had an incredible array of information about jazz people in the Caribbean (and beyond) and could at the shrug of his shoulder or in between ground dove nods of his head give you a list of jazz musicians or persons to contact.

It was Sco who influenced me into establishing the Barbados/Caribbean Jazz Festival in 1983. It was Sco's influence that defined that festival as a festival for Caribbean Jazz.

Sco was a gentleman and in all the years that I knew him I cannot remember him raising his voice once. He was always aware of the discussions on Caribbean musical culture, regardless of the conflicts over administration or the concepts of the music. He was a good listener and many took his humility and silence to be ignorance. Many missed the point. That was Sco's cool.

Scofield Pilgrim, a jazz institution of the Caribbean; gone, but remembered.

When I was a student in Canada in the late fifties, I was introduced to the character of the Bad John of Trinidad. And so the story was told of Gold Teet, the baddest of the bad and his hollow ground razor sweetened with garlic to stop the pain when the razor slash. Legend and ole talk.

And then in the late sixties, just as I was meeting Sco, I heard about the Jamaican Rude Bwoy and was soon to see Jimmy Cliff in *The Harder They Come*.

These were characters who showed little respect for society's rules and who demonstrated their disgust and contempt in antisocial behaviour until death terminated their wars.

In Barbados, we had a Bad John and a Rude Bwoy too. He was not a murderer, he was not a killer, but he was notorious for his disrespect for every icon and institution in the country.

He was known to have asked a white female magistrate in the most graphic of terms if she had carried out her morning ablutions before leaving home. In another court, he splattered the sitting magistrate with ripe feces collected in the folds of his short pants, an action that forced the abandonment of that court for days, if not weeks.

This Bajan rude bwoy spent more time in jail than outside. And it was prison that reformed him. He claimed that it was the cat (cat-o-nine tails whip) that made him alter his ways. His last job in prison was looking after the same cat and the gallows ropes.

I asked him why he behaved the way he did, why he stole and robbed stores. His answer was simple: "because they were there."

In the last decade and a half, he washed cars for a living and it was then that I discovered a completely different aspect of this man. I found out that he was a very avid reader, a keen observer of human kind, a very generous and gentle man, and a most astute political commentator.

Every year he celebrated his birthday with a party at his modest home in Beckles Road. The food, the drink, the talk were stimulants for his philosophical outpourings of common sense and wisdom. He detested injustice and would use his bad boy traits to support the underdog and to intimidate the wrongdoer. These were the stories he told. He bore no grudges, expressed no regrets of a life lived against the grain. He loved his friends and shared his wealth with them. I was a friend. Now, no more birthdays.

Gwenworkman was his mother. Cecil Workman was his name. I knew him as Swine.

The Merrymen:
A Caribbean Legacy

BAJANS WERE upset. They were aghast. They talked about those wutless people that make movies.

They were talking primarily 'bout Joan Collins who came to Barbados in the 1950s to film Alec Waugh's *Island in the Sun*. She was scandalous, it was said. She was bathing nude, naked as she born, in the sea pon a moonlight night with all them men including James Mason and Harry Belafonte. Decent people don't do that, especially white people. Bajans wanted to know where they get she from. How she had no class.

And after they left and the movie came out, we all flocked to Farley Hill to see the place which Hollywood chose to shoot their movie. Bajans were proud.

I remember going with my family on what I thought was my first visit only to be told by my mother that I had been there before. When? I certainly didn't remember. Then my mother told me that they took me there as a baby to some fair and how the place had a mahogany staircase like Marshall Hall and how I pull at the governor when he pass.

And then, the place burn down. I don't know how or why. A man called Bradshaw had owned it. I won't tell you what he grandson Boo Boo tell me how he get the money to buy it. But the government bought it. At one point Errol Barrow wanted to restore it, but it was too expensive an undertaking. It became a

National Park, eventually under the watchful and despotic eye of the late environmentalist, Iris Banochie.

I love Farley Hill. I love the ruins, with its blackened oversized soft-stone walls and its windowless sockets. I love its grounds, the natural amphitheatre with its Banyan framed proscenium stage.

Before the days of security guards, I spent many moonlit and moonless nights perched on the hill looking out across the Atlantic, savouring the salt breezes and timing the flashes of East Point Lighthouse. Obviously, there were other distractions, but not enough to sever my consciousness with where we were.

I used to look at those ruins when the moon was on high watching the reflections of the dew-damp fallen beams, forming silhouettes of some Shakespearean set. I used to dream of music drifting up from the little garden on the East Side of the ruins, down below where I lounged on the grass.

I had seen Duke Ellington and Herbie Mann and Miles Davis and Count Basie and Miriam Makeba and Ray Charles and many more at Columbia University's Lewisohm Stadium, at Forest Hills and in Central Park. I was fascinated with those summer concerts as a student in New York.

I dreamed of music at Farley Hill.

The opportunity to produce that music came in 1982/3 with the first of the Farley Hill Folk Concerts under the technical supervision of Annette Trotman, Dorsie Boyce and Maxie Baldeo.

There are two things I remember about that concert. The huge crowd and the Merrymen.

It was a logistics nightmare to get the public and private transport right. All traffic had to come from one direction and exit into the country from the other. In some cases, people had to walk from Speightstown, five miles away.

ROBIN HUNTE, EMILE STRAKER AND CHRIS GIBBS

Farley Hill itself had to be wrapped in BRC mesh wire to keep out potential stowaways. This was not as complex as its sounds, since it was only the eastern side that bordered the road that was to receive such treatment. The Park was bordered by a steep hill, fields of sugar canes and a deep dense forest of majestic mahogany trees. Only those from nearby villages who knew the tracks through the woods would try entering the Park from that way. A few did.

Many Bajans were critical of the Merrymen because of the colour thing. They felt that Emile Straker and the Merrymen got advantages over other musicians because of their colour. This point may have been true, but it was also evident from early that Emile Straker and Robin Hunte had done their homework on Barbadian folk music.

For example, Robin Hunte will forever remain the quintessential rhythm guitarist. His strumming on that four-string guitar drove the Merrymen's early performances. He learnt this art from a beach musician by the name of Sam who used to play along St. Lawrence Beach. He became part of that continuum out of Africa even though he wasn't African. I lamented that changing production values buried his guitar in the background rather than up front as it used to be.

Emile Straker, the artist, the writer, the composer. An incredible writer with wit to match and a sweet-sweet tenor voice that soared like a singing angel kite in an Easter Sky. Emile dug deep into the Bajan soundscape for the traditional songs that he made his own. His ear caught a phrase or two in the market or crowded streets or even at a race day at the Garrison Savannah and from these he knitted words into lyrics and waxed them with melodies for his countrymen and visitors alike.

Emile too, like Robin, built on the traditions that many felt that Barbados never had. But yet I hear in his guitar lines memories of Shilling and Lindy Bradshaw, two of Barbados' early street guitarists whose work started in the early 1920s. There are licks that they play that I have heard Emile play live and on record and that will now pass to future generations.

Bass player Chris Gibbs was unique. His complementary playing was both harmonic and rhythmic like a box-base (rumba box). His playing was like that of a drummer, with a tonal feeling. He was the first man I heard playing soca lines in the Merrymen's songs, long before it became known as soca. It was a style that evolved. He accentuated the pulse of the band, bearing in mind Robin's guitar work and that of the rest of the group.

When I booked Emile and the Merrymen that night at Farley Hill, I was going against the desires of that young crowd who wanted to hear the young Dub artists.

It was a black night of deep black clouds. Rain threatened.

It took only five minutes for the Merrymen to get the whole of Farley Hill jumping. After about half an hour, they slowed the tempo and told the tale of Sam Lord. Sam Lord was a pirate who slung lanterns on the coconut trees along the beach to deceive the ships into believing they had reached Bridgetown. The ships would sail towards the lights and run aground on the reefs from which Sam Lord would raid them.

As Emile's voice captured the now quieted audience with his romantic ballad, the sky broke and out popped this magnificent full moon flooding Farley Hill with a luminescence that brought a single audible gasp from the audience.

The Merrymen were magnificent that night. Songs that sounded staid on record became vibrant anthems of bacchanal. The crowd was ecstatic.

Last December, the Merrymen gave their final performance at the Sir Garfield Sobers Complex in Barbados after more than thirty years of performances. I was not there, but my heart was. The Merrymen was a pioneer group. They have never been challenged and have been masters of their genre, not only in Barbados, but in the whole Caribbean, the USA and Canada. They leave a legacy second to none.

Well done fellows, well done!

Saturday Night Fish Fry

Beaches, Signs and Omens

I DON'T know how Sharkey got his name, but for sure a shark had something to do with it. There was a time in Lower Carlton, St. James, when you could find sharks loitering in the surf.

Sharkey was a fisherman. He owned a moses that he used to pull up under the manchineel trees in front our bayhouse just north of St. Albans Anglican Church. We used to help him push it off and pull it up. He usually went out to sea early in the morning, sculling out to the point where he make a straight line wid Gibbes Point to the North and Church Point in Holetown to the South.

Sharkey would drop the big rock he used as an anchor. He would pull up the wire cages he called fish pots, cross them pon de bow and remove the chubs and snappers and ning-nings trapped inside.

Sharkey had a lot of fish pots and he had to search for them as the tides would shift them round. When yuh had heavy 'seven seas', it would take hours to find all the fish pots.

'Seven seas' were terrible churning, sucking waves that used to wash right up the beach and into the road in a series of seven waves with the last one being tumultuous. Yuh din mek sport with 'seven seas'. They suck out sand from the beach, sometimes leaving a mini-cliff some fourteen feet deep. Ask Elmer Jordan how tall he breakwater wall is. Elmer Jordan was a Speightstown businessman who build a big fancy bayhouse just North of us. He build this huge breakwater almost twenty feet high to protect his investment.

Many a manchineel tree toppled over and died in the sea from the excavating power of the 'seven seas'. Many mossy reefs were buried and many a moses that was left untied on the beach get way and drift out to sea. A next time, yuh see new reefs coming to the surface and the water get deep deep in some places.

'Seven seas' even laid bare the secrets of St. Albans burial grounds, exposing the skulls and bones of cholera victims, long forgotten, because no one could remember which cholera epidemic put them there.

The old people could remember though, when the reefs at St. Albans Point made up the official burial ground. The 'seven seas' thought that St. Albans was too small to have a graveyard on the beach and take way all de sand and left a bare black rocky reef for cobblers and sea eggs.

Today the beach at Lower Carlton is wide and expansive and manicured. No turtle trails, no turtle eggs. No rotting matter to keep frays and pilchards and jacks in the surf. No more net casters or seine boats. No shaggas in the moss. No moss. Just crystal clear waters.

And who owns the beach?

Over the last three to four decades, there has been an alteration of Barbados' beaches brought about by the development of the Bridgetown Port, the Coast Guard Station at Oistins, the Hilton Hotel, the Fisherman's Harbour at Hincks Street and the numerous illegal structures along the West Coast.

Last week, Sandy Lane's hired gun wrote of the law, engineers and high and low water marks and signs (he left out omens). These new expansive beaches no more belong to the owners of the land adjacent to the beaches than they belong to the sea.

There is a church off Maxwell Coast Road whose congregation each Sunday is entirely made up of fish, eels and cobblers. The sea claimed it many many years ago. Similarly, Worthing Beach was once the domain of the rich and powerful.

There is a saying "leave well enough alone." Mr. Barry Gale, legal counsel to the Sandy Lane Property Owners Association and the Sandy Lane property owners should know that signs come with omens. Bajans respect private property, but will not accept that property owners, especially Sandy Lane property owners, have a special treaty with the Lord, to be the only beneficiaries of his work.

The late former Prime Minister of Barbados, Errol Barrow, was fond of reminding Bajans that "the Lord giveth and the Lord taketh away." Gabby, on the other hand, warned us in *Jack* to remember that our navel strings are buried here.

Don't mess with the Lord or Bajans when it comes to our beaches! Whatever can happen, can happen here. Beware.

Saturday Night Fish Fry

"You don't have to pay the usual admission
If you are a cook or a waiter or a good musician
So if you happen to be just passing by
Stop in at the Saturday Night Fish Fry."

Louis Jordan and his Tympany Five

MARTIN'S BAY is like a loop, a loop that curls like a noose to knot a shallow beach between a black scarred reef and a black macadam road. Potted once upon a time in the sands were singularly lean coconut trees to shelter this fragile loop of beach in a speckled shade. That was a time when fishing boats had sails. A distant loop from a distant past where the sea salt blinded ambition.

And Martin's Bay people always lingered in my mind as having a sense of privacy that was uniquely their own. There wasn't much land, but what there was land it was planted with bay houses and homes held precariously together by rust and paint.

Martin's Bay is an outpost. As far from the tourist industry as imagination can make. Not interesting enough to force the tourist buses down the loop. Not even to see the remnants of a long gone train or to hear the strains of the mythical and mystical Brumley band hiding in the wind.

Martin's Bay today is sedate and settled, but how I would like to see a Martin's Bay Saturday Night Fish Fry on the slender beach, replete with Sam Lord's lanterns and Julian Hunte bonfires, roast breadfruit, fried plantain, potato pickings (the extra sweet potatoes) and other delights.

In a two-by-four island like ours, everything counts. There should be no wasteland. Tourism has developed as an industry far removed from the rest of us. It was precious to a few, hoteliers by and large, who saw their properties as oases in a desert of primitive yahoos. And who used to get every concession, tax free holidays as if they did tourist themselves, tourist from taxes. And to some others the historical sojourn in plantation houses with silver forks was touted as the 'places to see'.

As far as planners and developers expect, we are to be the hewers of wood and carry water buckets on our heads forever. And regardless of how sophisticated everything appears in Barbados, there are now some sophisticated hewers of wood and some sophisticated water bucket carriers.

What I am driving at here is the absence of real benefits to black Bajans. Somehow I get the impression that we are still getting the pickings from the fields of tourism. The pickings from a field of sweet potatoes, those premature finger-sized potatoes that were usually good for feeding hogs. When roasted and served with raw salt fish and washed down by a frothy-head mauby, served as food for many of our parents.

And much of it seems to be our fault, it is said.

We have a billion-dollar tourism industry and seem to feel that it should operate on automatic pilot. For the Concorde class, of course—there are real estate permits and pathways to heaven; for we must dress-up in our Sunday go-to-meetings and stand-up outside like our parents used to do outside the Marine Hotel pon old year's night.

Exactly what must we do to get noticed, to get fair treatment? Get it straight, I talking bout those who get scratch grain scatter in their path like if dem is starve out bare-neck fowls.

We don't have to bend down.

Tourism is valid and all Bajans who want to be in it must be in it. Some can't or don't know what the product is and some do. Some can't suck the sweet and the rest suck salt. It cyan be that. It ent to say that some of we ent there. Some of we there. And that is why the rest of we want to get in too. Some cyan have and the rest ent to have.

Everybody got beach and sand and de sun, if the devil and he wife don't fight fuh de coocoo stick too often and too long. But Buhbadus is we, all of we and all of wunna. Everything that get pack up and send down the line to we from we father and mother father and mother is what is Bajan. So it just cyan be for some of we and not the rest.

Martin's Bay got people that does fish for a living. Them know every fishing ground from Martin's Bay to the Cow and the Calf and the Horse Nostril right through to the Bowbells. So why them can't get piece of the action offering sea tours? Is only imported bus that is to get use?

Culture is what people do in a particular environment. It different. So what wrong with Martin's Bay people? Them ent to live and enjoy the sweets too?

So Martin's Bay, don't wait. Light up the coalpots and the smut lamps and fry some fish pon a Sarduh night. Yuh don't have to pay the usual admission. Forget the scratch grain.

Da Beach is mine too!

"Da beach is mine!"

The Mighty Gabby

I AM currently in the middle of a study for the Office of the Prime Minister looking at the development of Festivals and Events in Jamaica. The mandate for this study is guided by the premise that more Jamaicans need to be involved in the benefits of tourism.

The full study requires our team to develop a plan for greater utilization of Heritage products, and for deepening the involvement of the wider community in all aspects of tourism—local and international.

What is clear from several studies that I have read is that the industry developed over the years as an elitist industry built around the provision of accommodation. The rest of the society was limited to being suppliers of certain services, or to peripheral contacts. This conforms to how the industry developed in Barbados as well as in the rest of the Caribbean. And of course sun, sea and sand became the holy grail that was offered to visitors from all around the world. This led to attempts to develop private beaches in order to keep the 'natives' out. It is still a major bone of contention by those owning hotels and there is always some attempt to erect artificial barriers to block out any encroachment by the 'natives'.

Sun, sea and sand are no longer the major reasons why people are travelling or selecting destinations. Many destinations are offering sun, sea and sand, so there have to be other factors that distinguish one destination from the next. Those factors are centred around the culture of the country/destination.

So it becomes part of the marketing strategy to look at heritage, natural and man-made, and all the other factors that make one tourism destination distinct from another. Thus, festivals and events can and do play a major role in the evolving strategies of tourism development. I think Barbados understands this, and in recent years it has been capitalizing on its heritage, its festivals and its events.

But how much do Barbadians benefit from this? That heritage belongs to all Barbados, but do we all benefit?

Jamaica wants to develop an internal tourism encouraging Jamaicans to explore their country in the most intimate of ways, participating in festivals and events of every description—agricultural, food, music, sports, heritage, etc.

I remember when the Barbados Transport Board introduced Sunday Excursions. I thought then that it was a marvelous idea and suggested to the then PRO, Stetson Babb, that it should have been connected to walking tours to give participants a better understanding of their country. There are several groups and individuals who understand Barbados very well and who, I am quite sure, would participate.

One of the fears expressed by tour operators in Barbados who opposed these excursions was that tourists would take those tours because they were cheaper. A pricing differential was proposed where visitors would have to pay a premium, but I believe that whoever wants to take the tours should be allowed to. Many visitors are now coming from our sister islands. I am sure they would enjoy the interaction with Bajan families on these excursions.

Many years ago, if memory serves me right, both Errol Barrow and Frank Walcott spoke about internal tourism and that Bajans should consider spending time in Bajan hotels instead of visiting the USA for vacations. Although the idea was a good one, many Bajans rejected it because it was never marketed to them in a meaningful way.

FRANK WALCOTT

Caribbean people have generally ignored the Caribbean market as a valid source for visitors. Somehow we do not regard ourselves as tourists when we visit our sister territories. And because our friends and family do not stay in hotels, generally they are not considered part of the tourism statistics.

ERROL BARROW

With the advent of the Caribbean Common Market, I expect that we are going to see increased activity in this area. Barbados is the leading destination for intra-Caribbean travellers. Jamaica has paid little attention to the Eastern Caribbean in the past, and vice versa, but it enjoys one of best relationships with its citizens in the diaspora. The remittances for family support provided by these prodigal sons and daughters are legendary and remain a major force in financial planning in the country.

However, in spite of its difficulties, Jamaica still has one of the richest and most varied of heritage tourism products. Physically you can find in Jamaica a replica of all of the Caribbean islands. And now there is an all-out thrust to make sure that all Jamaicans become beneficiaries of this very explosive industry.

It is truly an interesting time and I will share in the future some of the creative solutions that are coming forth from the people themselves. Jamaicans too are beginning to understand that "da beach is mine."

Paradise Lost?

I WAS told to be at Paradise Beach Club by eight o' clock that night and to meet him by the bar. I was there. My old school mate Oliver Broomes (Lord Radio) was in fine form on the bandstand. He had four bands, all called The Bimshire Boys, working simultaneously at four different hotels. He sang for

about thirty minutes and then he was off to do the same at another venue. He would be back for the floor show that featured a belly dancer, a fire eating act and the limbo.

LORD RADIO

Paradise Beach Club was the perfect spot. It was nestled under the escarpment of the Black Rock ledge with a beautiful beach that gurgled pure, cool, fresh water in the surf. There is a legend that two ducks were released in Cole's Cave in St. Thomas to swim in the underground river. One of the ducks allegedly came out in Long Pond, St. Andrew, and the other at Freshwater Beach or Paradise Beach as it is now called.

Paradise was not always a paradise for Black Bajans when it was Freshwater Hotel. You could bathe at Spring Garden/Pile Bay and Brighton Beach to the South or at Batts Rock to the North. Freshwater beach was a no-no. You could walk along the beach, but you were not to pause, linger, or languish in the bubbling cool waters.

In recent years, you don't see a lot of this gurgling water anymore and one suspects that what little is left from the over-consumption by Bajans is used by Barbados Light and Power to cool down their turbines. The desalination plant will probably suck off the rest to convert to fresh water for us to drink.

Paradise was the place to be. There was always good entertainment. The Merrymen were also regulars weekly and many bands tried to be part of the entertainment there. It attracted a lot of Canadian and American women who outnumbered by far the men that came to Barbados in those days. So with all of this honey around, the hustlers were in full flower.

I was to be shown the art of hustling by a specialist in the field. My instructor was a successful pro who knew the runnings.

First, he said, you looked to see if the ladies have a suntan. If they did, it was likely that they had been in the island more than a day and were likely to have been picked up by someone else. Professional ethics only allowed you to make a note just in case a disagreement developed. In such cases you had to observe to see if there was any inactivity.

Next, you checked to see what kind of cigarettes they were smoking. Parliament or Marlboros would indicate that they were Americans. Du Maurier or Export A or Rothmans would suggest Canadians. Americans were more likely to be prejudiced, so caution had to exercised. That is, you did a little bit more talking to get a full picture. Canadians were almost a certainty.

My pro friend then drew my attention to their feet. If the feet were tapping to the music, it suggested that they would like to dance and so you could make your move. Many a Bajan learned to master the two-step. If the ladies were in a group of two or three or four, you had to form an alliance with some other hustlers before you made your move. One on one guaranteed success, as it was easier to move away from the group.

It is interesting to note that this was the first time that I saw Bajan black and white men cooperating and socializing together. All barriers drop when a hustle is in play. Since women come in all colours, sizes, shapes, looks and ages, there are specialists for each of these categories. Those who waited like gaulins for the remnants were given names like 'Stuff Cart'.

Paradise Beach Club was a happy hunting ground for many and it is interesting to note that many of these hustlers who approached their work as pros, have been able to acquire land and build houses from the sale of their services.

Perhaps Butch Stewart knows these runnings. His all-inclusives do not include such services as yet. But whenever he chooses, if ever, to reopen Paradise, the Bajan Adams will be offering Eves pendulous golden apples in the Garden of Eden. But in this day and age though, Butch may just be butch.

Acronyms

AC	Anglican Church
ADM	Arthur Daniel Midlands
AG	Attorney General
aka	also known as
BARTEL	Barbados Telephone Company now part of the Cable and Wireless Group
BCA	Barbados Cricket Association
BET	Barbados External Communications now part of the Cable and Wireless Group
BFA	Barbados Football Association
BG	British Guiana, now Guyana
BICO	Barbados Ice Company and also a brand name for their ice cream
BIDC	Barbados Industrial Development Corporation
BIMAP	Barbados Institute of Management and Productivity
BLP	Barbados Labour Party
BNB	Barbados National Bank
B&P	Business and Professional Women's Club, and American social organization
BRC	Blue Rhythm Combo a popular Bajan band of the 1960s and 1970s. It is also the name of a company that manufactures steel mesh.
BS&T	Barbados Shipping and Trading
BSTU	Barbados Secondary School Teachers Union

BUT	Barbados Union of Teachers
BWIA	British West Indies Airways - the original name of BWEE
CANA	Caribbean News Agency
CARICOM	Caribbean Community and Common Market
CARIFESTA	Caribbean Festival of Arts
CARIFTA	Caribbean Free Trade Area
CBC	Caribbean Broadcasting Corporation, a statutory corporation owned by the government of Barbados and operates CBC-TV, Radio 900, and Radio Liberty
CBC-TV	Caribbean Broadcasting Company Television
CBU	Caribbean Broadcasting Union
CC	Codrington College
CCN	Caribbean Cable News, Trinidad
CEO	Chief Executive Officer
CIA	Central Intelligence Agency, USA
CIB	Criminal Investigation Bureau of the Jamaica Constabulary Force (Police)
CIBC	The former Canadian Imperial Bank of Commerce which amalgamated with Barclays Bank PLC to form First Caribbean Bank
CLICO	Colonial Life Insurance Company, a Trinidad family owned insurance company that operates in the Eastern Caribbean and the Guyanas
CMA	Caribbean Music Awards
CNN	Cable News Network, USA
CONCACAF	Confederation of North, Central America and Caribbean Football
CPBA	Caribbean Publishers and Broadcasters Association
CPR	Canadian Pacific Railway

CSN	A television station owned by a Jamaican operating out of Miami in the mid 1990s.
CTO	Caribbean Tourism Organization
CVM-TV	A Jamaican television station
C&W	Cable and Wireless
CXC	Caribbean Examinations Council
D&G	Desnoes and Geddes, a beverage manufacturing company in Jamaica
DLP	Democratic Labour Party
DPP	Director of Public Prosecutions
FINSAC	Financial Sector Adjustment Company Limited - a government statutory corporation established to bail out bankrupt companies)
GBS	Guyana Broadcasting System
GCT	General Consumption Tax
GEM	The name of a FM radio network operating out of Ohio, USA on satellite to stations in several of the islands of the Eastern Caribbean. These operations started in the 1980s
GULP	Grenada United Labour Party
HRD	Human Resource Director
ICC	International Cricket Council
IMF	International Monetary Fund
INTEL	An American electronics firm that manufactures various computer parts
JBC	Jamaica Broadcasting Corporation, a statutory corporation owned by the government of Jamaica. The television station and one radio station was sold to private interest
JCF	Jamaica Constabulary Force
JFF	Jamaica Football Federation
JLP	Jamaica Labour Party

JPSCo	Jamaica Public Service Company
JTA	Jamaica Teachers' Association
LIAT	Leeward Islands Air Transport, an airline linking the islands of the Eastern Caribbean
MCC	Marylebone Cricket Club, the original organization managing cricket in the UK
NCF	National Cultural Foundation, Barbados
NDM	National Democratic Movement, Jamaica
NEMWIL	An Eastern Caribbean general insurance company headquartered in Trinidad
NIFCA	National Independence Festival of the Creative Arts held in Barbados during October and November each year and culminating at Independence, November 30.
NRG	National Results Graph
NTG	National Theoretical Graph
NWC	National Water Commission, Jamaica
OECS	Organization of Eastern Caribbean States whose administrative headquarters is in Castries, St. Lucia
PNM	People's National Movement, Trinidad and Tobago
PNP	People's National Party, Jamaica
PSOJ	Private Sector Organization of Jamaica
QRC	Queen's Royal College, Trinidad
RCMP	Royal Canadian Mounted Police, Canada
RJR	Radio Jamaica and Rediffusion, Jamaica (Radio Jamaica Limited)
SAT	Scholastic Aptitude Test - required for admission to American Colleges and Universities
SEC	Securities Exchange Commission, Barbados
SPG	Society for the Propagation of the Gospel

SWOT	Strengths Weaknesses Opportunities Threats
UCWI	University College of the West Indies
UFO	Unidentified Flying Object
UNIA	Universal Negro Improvement Association
UWI	University of the West Indies
WIBC	West Indies Cricket Board
WICI	West Indies Cricket Incorporated
WIFLP	West Indian Federal Labour Party
WIPA	West Indies Players Association (Cricket)

Notes

Adams, Jimmy: Jamaican born West Indian cricketer. Former Captain of the West Indies Team

Adams, Grantley: Founder of the Barbados Labour Party. First Premier of Barbados and First and only Prime Minister of the West Indies Federation

Allman, Chris: Barbadian keyboard player and music producer.

Babb, Fielding: Barbadian artist

Bailey, Donovan: Jamaican born Canadian athlete who was disqualified at the Seoul Olympics for using enhancement drugs

Bailey, MacDonald: Outstanding Trinidadian sprinter of the 1940s

Banja: Any rhythmic secular Bajan music but primarily music played by Bumbatuk bands.

Banton, Buju: Jamaican Dancehall singer

Barbados Landship Movement: A social organisation based on the structure of British Navy of the 19th Century but in reality a crucible of African cultural retentions

Barrow, Errol: Founder of the Democratic Labour Party in Barbados. Prime Minister of Barbados from 1961-1976 and 1986-87. Died in office

Belafonte, Harry: Renown Jamaican born folk singer

Belleplaine: A small town on the Eastern coast of Barbados

Best, Willie: A black American actor

Bishop, Son Son: A Bumbatuk drummer in Barbados

Blackett, Andrea: A young Barbadian athlete

Bourne, London: A former slave who became a wealthy black businessman during the period of slavery in Barbados. He owned several plantations and properties in Bridgetown. The equivalent of the Chamber of Commerce used to meet in one of his buildings but he was not allowed to become a member.

Bovell, Dennis: A Barbadian born London based music producer who goes by the name of Blackbeard

Bradman: Don Bradman, the great Australian cricketer

Brathwaite, Edward Kamau: The brilliant Barbadian poet and cultural guru

Brewster Brothers: Harold and Lisle. A family known for their athletic prowess. Lived in Hindsbury Road, Bridgetown

Broodhagen, Karl: Guyanese born Barbadian sculptor and teacher. Creator of Bussa, Grantley Adams and Gary Sobers monuments.

Brown, Carl: Jamaican coach of the Reggae Boys, the Jamaican Football team.

Bumbatuk Music: The traditional folk music of Barbados

Bum Drum: The large bass drum used in Bumbatuk music

Burnham, Forbes: Founder of the Peoples Progressive Party (PPP) with Cheddi Jagan in Guyana later formed Peoples National Congress (PNC)after split with Jagan and was long serving Prime Minister of Guyana until is death.

Bussa Awards: The first awards to recognize the contribution of Barbadians to the cultural development of Barbados. Named after Bussa, the leader of the 1816 slave revolt. Was established by Yoruba Yard

Busta: The name of a soft drink manufactured in Trinidad and Tobago

Bustamante, Alexander: The popular Jamaican Trade Unionist and political leader known as Busta who founded the

Bustamante Industrial Trades Union (BITU) and the Jamaica Labour Party (JLP). Was Prime Minister of Jamaica.

Carlton: A sports club in Black Rock, St. Michael, Barbados where colour played a major role in recruitment of membership

Carter, Anthony Gabby: The Barbadian calypsonian, the Mighty Gabby, winner of several calypso competitions

Cave Shepherd: A department store on Broad Steer, Bridgetown, Barbados

Challenor, George: A white Barbadian cricketer of the 1920s and 30s who was a legendary opening batsmen

Christie, Linford: A Jamaican born London based athlete

Clarke, A.C.: An imaginative writer of Science fiction. An American

Clarke, Bobby: A Barbadian Marxist lawyer and political activist

Compton Dennis: An English cricket batsman of the 1940s and 50s

Congaline Festival: A pre-Crop Over Festival started by the band Spice and now organized by the government thru the National Cultural Foundation

Cooper, Gary: Hollywood actor

C.O. Williams: Sir Charles O Williams, a road builder and land developer in Barbados

Crabbe, Buster: A Hollywood actor who played early Tarzan in the movies

Crop Over: The annual major festival in Barbados held during the months of June and July and culminating on the first Monday of August

deportees: A reference to persons sent back to Jamaica primarily by the US and Canadian governments but is also used to describe used vehicles imported from Japan.

don: A leader/enforcer in a community

Donkey Belly: A costumed character found dancing with a

Bumbatuk Band

eleven plus: An exam taken by students within the age group of 11+ to determine which secondary schools they will be allocated to

Eunice: Karl Broodhagen's wife

Farnum, Ken: A popular Barbadian cyclist of the 1940s and 1950s who went to the Olympics in 1952

Federation: The West Indies Federation which was abandoned when Jamaican decided in a referendum to withdraw

Fetchit, Steppin: A black American actor who played many Uncle Tom roles in the movies

Forde Brothers: Harold and Courtenay. Members of a distinguished black Bajan family

Four Square Affair: A group of Plantations in the parish of St. Phillip that were put up for sale by the mortgagee. A black family made what was a winning bid but because of a series of machinations outside of their control they were sold to a white group who came in at the eleventh hour.

garrison community: A community or constituency in Jamaica which is controlled by a political party.

Garvey, Marcus: One of the world's outstanding visionaries who was born in Jamaica

Gittens, Anne: A highly qualified Barbadian woman who is both an engineer and a chartered accountant. Was a Director of the Barbados Mutual

Glendairy: The name of the main prison in Barbados

Goddard, JN: A poor white from the parish of St. John in Barbados who founded the firm J N Goddard and Sons Ltd

Goddard, Sir John Stanley: A grandson of J N Goddard and former Chairman of Goddards

Gollop, Sir Fred: A lawyer and former journalist who is Chairman of the Nation Group and President of the Senate in Barbados

Gordon, Flash: A Barbadian boxer in the 1950s

Griffith, Joseph: An outstanding Barbadian musician who served as the leader of military bands in St. Lucia, Martinique and Trinidad in the 1930s thru to the 1950s. Established and took on tour to Europe the first steelband, the Trinidad All Stars Percussion Orchestra (TASPO)

Grundig sets: A German made radio receiver

Guillen, Nicholas: Cuban poet

Headley, George: One of the great pre-World War II West Indian cricketers. Born in Panama of a Barbadian father and a Jamaican mother, he was raised in Jamaica and played for Jamaica.

Hemmings, Deon: A Jamaican Olympic gold medalist in athletics

His Master's Voice: The logo of the American company Radio Corporation of America (RCA)

Holt: J.K. Holt, a Jamaican test cricketer of the 1950s

Hooper: Carl Hooper, Guyanese born Captain of the West Indies team

Hoyte, Harold: Editor-in-Chief of the Nation Newspapers, Barbados

Hunte, K. R.: A white Barbadian businessman, prominent in the 1960s and 1970s

Hylton: Leslie Hylton, a Jamaican who was convicted of murder when J K Holt was playing for the West Indies during the 1950s

Issa, John: The Jamaican hotelier

Jab-Jab: A traditional masquerade dance from Trinidad carnival

Jackman, Oliver: A prominent Barbadian lawyer, human rights activist, journalist and former diplomat

Jagan, Cheddi: East Indian Guyanese co-founder with the

African Forbes Burnham of the Peoples Political Party and then Prime Minister of Guyana

Jamaican Quartet: The most famous of Caribbean athletes, the Jamaicans Herb McKenley, Arthur Wint, George Rhoden and Les Laing who won the Gold Medal in the 4 x 400 relay at the 1952 Olympics in Helsinki

James, C.L.R.: The outstanding Trinidadian intellectual and author.

Job, Morgan: The Tobago born academic who was a iconoclastic talk show host before becoming a Minister in the Basdeo Panday government

Kamau: Edward Kamau Brathwaite, the Barbadian poet and cultural guru

Kasavubu: The first President of the Congo before he was removed in a coup by General Mobutu. He became President for a second time and was again removed by Mobutu in another coup

King, Horace: A Barbadian land surveyor and former cricketer

Kittie: The smallest drum in a Bumbatuk Band which is outfitted with snares and buzzes and is played on the hip

Ladd, Allan: An American movie star

Laing, Arthur: An outstanding Jamaican quarter miler.

Lamming, George: One of Barbados great political thinkers and writers. Author of several novels.

Landship: A social organization that is a crucible of African dance retention among other things (Landship Movement)

Lara, Brian: Trinidadian born West Indies cricketer and holder of highest score in test cricket

Lashley, Beverly: Former Deputy-Director of the National Cultural Foundation

Leacock, Leo and Company: A Barbadian businessman

Lee Ralph, Sheryl: Jamaican actress in the movies and on television in USA and founder of the Jamerican Film Festival

Legs Arthur: A Barbados born railway porter on the Canadian railways

Leon, Madame Rose: A Jamaican politician and ally of Sir Alexander Bustamante

Lewis, Sir Arthur: St. Lucian born Nobel Laureate, economist and former Vice-Chancellor of the University of the West Indies

Lewis, Eric: A member of the satirical group MADD and the main writer and composer of its music

Lightbourne, Robert: Jamaican industrialist and member of Jamaica Labour Party

Lloyd, Clive: Guyanese born West Indies cricketer and former captain of the West Indies team

Lynch, Louis: A Barbadian teacher, writer and politician (former Mayor of Bridgetown) who was also the proprietor of a very successful private school, the Modern High School

Lumumba: Patrice Lumumba was Prime Minister of the Congo Democratic Republic when it gained independence from Belgium in June 1960. By June 1963, he was murdered.

Manley, Edna: The wife of the Jamaican National Hero Norman Washington Manley and mother of Michael Manley. An outstanding woman in her own right, she was a sculptor of great significance

Manley, Michael: Former Prime Minister of Jamaica

Manley, Norman: Former Premier of Jamaica and founder of the Peoples National Party

Marley, Robert Nesta: The world renowned reggae singer

McKenley, Herb: An outstanding Jamaican quarter miler

Miller, Freddie: Former Minister in the Barbados Labour Party government and from a family of industrialists

Minshall, Peter: The Trinidad born carnival costume designer who works on major international projects like the Olympics Opening ceremonies

Moreland, Mantan: A black American movie actor

Morgan Lewis: A plantation in St. Andrew on the East Coast of Barbados and has one of the last working windmills that grind cane to produce sugar

Mr. Harding: An effigy made by stuffing cane trash (dried cane leaves) into old clothes. This effigy was called Mr Harding and came to symbolize, after Emancipation, the coming of Hard Times i.e. the period when employment on the plantation was lowest

Naipaul, V. S.: The Trinidad born Nobel Laureate for literature

Nancy story: Anancy story

Nazi: The nickname of a Barbadian cyclist who had more heart than ability

Nicholas: Nicholas Brancker, a musician and pioneering producer of contemporary Bajan music

Norville, Don: A former Sports Editor with the Barbados Advocate

Ovaltine: A chocolate based drink

Ottey, Merlene: An outstanding Jamaican born female sprinter

Peck, Gregory: An American movie actor

Panday: Basdeo Panday, the former Prime Minister of Trinidad and Tobago

Penny Whistle/fife: A Flute

Perse, Saint-John: Marie Renee Auguste Alexis Leeger, 1960 Nobel Laureate poet from Guadeloupe

Pickwick: A cricket club in Barbados whose membership policies was based on skin colour

Phillips: The brand name of a Dutch electronics firm

Pollock Brothers: Two world class South African cricketers

Poonka: The calypso name of Wayne Willock

Potato Mout: The nickname of an outstanding Bumbatuk drummer

Poitier, Sidney: Oscar winning actor from the Bahamas

Powell, Colin: The Jamaican born former Chief of Staff of the US Armed Forces and Secretary of State

Primus, Pearl: Trinidadian dancer and choreographer and anthropologist

Queensbury or Johnson rules: European stick fighting rules

Radiogram: A radio and record player combination unit that was built as a piece of furniture

Ramadhin: Trinidadian born bowler Sonny Ramadhin who mesmerized England in 1950 with his Jamaica partner Alf Valentine

Red Stripe: The name of a Jamaican beer

Red Stripe Bowl: One time trophy of supremacy in West Indies Cricket

Reggae Boyz: The name given to the Jamaican Football team during its campaign to get to France in 1998

Rhoden, George: An outstanding Jamaican quarter miler

Richards, Viv (Sir): The Antiguan born former Captain of the awesome West Indies Cricket team that ruled world cricket for 17 years. Himself a formidable batsmen who was called by the press as the Master Blaster

Richardson, Richie: Antiguan born former Captain of the West Indies cricket team.

Ring Bang: A type of music developed by the Guyanese Eddy Grant based on Caribbean traditional rhythms

Roett, John: A Barbadian musician and producer

Rohlehr, Gordon: Guyanese born UWI Professor (St. Augustine) who has written extensively on Caribbean culture especially Trinidad calypso

Rousseau: Pat Rousseau, a Jamaica lawyer and former President of the West Cricket Board

Seaman: Name of the popular flute player in a Bumbatuk Band

Scott, Randolph: An American movie star of Westerns

Seale, R. L.: The name of a distribution company in Barbados

Shaggy Bear: A masquerade costume character associated with Bumbatuk Bands in Barbados

Short, Peter: A white Barbadian former President of the Barbados Cricket Association and a member of the West Indies Cricket Board

Sir John: Sir John Stanley Goddard

sketels: A description given fast loose women and also to a type of Japanese used cars used as robot taxis in Jamaica

Skinner, John: A former champion cyclist in Barbados

Sobers, Gary: The greatest cricketer the world has ever known. Great all-rounder - batting, bowling, fielding. Former Captain of the West Indies team, he held the highest score in test cricket for about 30 years before it was broken by Lara. A Barbados National Hero

Spice: The name of a former music group out of Barbados

Spin Twins: Ramadhin and Valentine

Springer, Sir Hugh: A former Governor-General of Barbados

Stewart, Butch: The Jamaican tourism head of Sandals hotels and Air Jamaica

Stewart, Omowale: A Barbadian artists and costume designer

Stewart and Sampson: A former trading company in Roebuck Street, Bridgetown in the first half of the 20th Century

Stone, Carl: The late Jamaican pollster who gave his name to the major polls in Jamaica

Straker, Emile: Lead singer in the Barbadian group the Merrymen

Taylor, Ralph: Chairman of the Almond Resorts Group in Barbados

The 3 Ws: The three revered Barbadian batsmen in the West Indies team from the late 1940s to the 1960s: Sir Frank Worrell (former Captain), Sir Everton Weekes and Sir Clyde Walcott

The two Richards: Richard Hoad and Richard Goddard, two white Bajan environmentalists

Thompson, Obadele: Young Barbadian Olympic class sprinter and Bronze medalist

Tiltman: A person who walks and dances on stilts

Ting: A Jamaican grapefruit flavoured softdrink

Trotman, Leroy: Now Sir Roy Trotman. General Secretary of the Barbados Workers Union (BWU)

Tshombe: Leader of a the breakaway state of Katanga in the Congo shortly after Independence and said to have been supported by Western interests

Tudor, Cammie: Deputy Prime Minister in the Democratic Labour Party (DLP) government

Tudor, James A.: A fascinating self-made businessman and father of Cammie Tudor

Tuk Band: Another name for the traditional Bumbatuk Band

Tull, Louis: A lawyer, member of Parliament and a former Attorney General and Minister of Foreign Affairs in the Barbados Labour Party (BLP) government under Tom Adams

Valentine, Alf: Left-arm Jamaican cricketer and spin bowler who with the Trinidadian Sonny Ramadhin formed the spin twins that mesmerized England in 1950

Virgil: Virgil Broodhagen, son of Karl and a painter and sculptor in his own right

Walcott, Sir Clyde: Outstanding Barbados and West Indies cricketer. One of the three Ws

Walcott, Derek: St. Lucian born poet and playwright who won the Nobel Prize for literature

Walcott, Sir Frank: The former powerful General Secretary of the Barbados Workers Union, head of the Caribbean Congress of Labour , and a former member of Parliament. A National Hero of Barbados

Walsh: Courtney Walsh, the Jamaican born former Captain of the West Indies team and holder of the world record for the most wickets in Test cricket

Wanderers: A cricket club in Barbados whose membership policy was based on colour.

Ward, A.F.: The scion of a plantation empire in the North of Barbados in the Parish of St. Lucy and the original manufacturer of Mount Gay Rum

Warrens Group: Companies owned or controlled by the family of Sir Charles O Williams

Waterman, Justice Frederick: A Barbadian judge

Wedderburn, Jim: A former Olympic athlete from Barbados

Weekes, Sir Everton: Outstanding Barbados and West Indies cricketer. One of the three Ws

Weismuller, Johnny: An American movie star who played the role of Tarzan in the movies and who was also an Olympic swimmer

Williams, Eric: Dr Eric Williams, long serving former Prime Minister of Trinidad and Tobago

Williams, Justices Sir Denys and Colin: Two bothers from a distinguished Barbadian family who served at the same time as judges in the Barbados Court, with Sir Denys as Chief Justice

Windward: A cricket club in Barbados whose membership policy was based on colour

Wint, Arthur: A Jamaican outstanding quarter miler

Worrell, Sir Frank: Outstanding Barbados and West Indies cricketer. One of the three Ws

Wuking up: Dancing

Yoruba/Yoruba Yard: A cultural organization founded by the author in the early 1970s

Zeeks: A Jamaican inner-city community leader

Glossary

akee — guinep not to be confused with Jamaican ackee

Anancy stories — Folk tales about Brer Anancy, a cunning spider of West African origin and other animals.

bacchanal — A very noisy merry-making; noisy fun (often with strong sexual overtones. @ Richard Allsopp

bad johns — bad men, sometime criminals. Gordon Rohlehr believes the term may be a 19th Century corruption by French creole speakers of the word Bajan (Barbadians)

Banja — all Bajan traditional music especially those songs with strong African rhythms

Baobab — African tree of which there are only three in Barbados

barrow a boar — Castrating a young male pig (a boar)

bassa-bassa — Trouble, noisy disagreement and confusion (Allsopp) Known as kas-kas in Jamaica

big-foot — Smart, avaricious

Bim — An African (Igbo) word meaning our people used to refer to Barbados and Bajans

blackguarding — Loud scurrilous language and aggressive

	behaviour (Allsopp)
blenzers	money
bo	Short for brother
bosie	A more musical form of bo
botsie	Bottom, backside
About whuh gine long	about what's happening
brakesing	stopping
brek dem foot	Bad luck, obeah. Impediments to progress are seen as someone working obeah to stop that progress
bruggadung	An echo word reflecting something falling and breaking with a loud noise
Buhbadus	Barbados
bull-cow	A male cow
bullers	Male homosexuals
bull pistle	The dried stretched penis of a bull-cow used as a whip
Bum, bumbatuk, bum drum	All related to music played by drum and kettle and fife preferably referred to as bumbatuk
bottoms	Depressions in cane fields where ponds would form after heavy rainfall
buy from dey mudda like goat	Young country girls from the Asmall@ islands were purchased from their mothers. The girls were then turned into prostitutes by the purchaser who invariably ran a hotel (whore

house) in Bridgetown

cane-fires	Fires set accidentally and deliberately of cane fields to force immediate reaping
careenage	An inner shallow harbour where schooners could be leaned to one side (careen) to allow for cleaning. Called carenage in Trinidad and Grenada
cassareep(ed)	AA thick, dark-brown liquid resembling molasses, produced by boiling down the juice squeezed from grated BITTER-CASSAVA to remove poison, and used to make and preserve pepperpot.@ Allsopp
chattel-house	A small timber house of a specific design capable of expansion like a railway train and can be moved from one location to another
chossel	A friend who is a sweetheart or love
clammacherry tree	A tree with very flexible branches which bears a pinkish fruit the size of a small grape. The flesh of the fruit is sticky and is used as a glue by children.
coalpot	a small shall outdoor stove shaped like a large champagne glass that uses coals. It is made of cast iron or pottery
coocoo stick	a stick shaped like a small cricket bat or paddle about 15 inches long but flat on both sides and is used to stir coocoo or turn cornmeal
cornmeal pap 'cream-o-wheat'	A porridge made from corn meal

flute	The opening phrase played by the flute in a Bumbatuk band imitating the sound of the phrase Acream of wheat@
cubbas	A vulture, john crow, gaulin
cyan	Can or can't, depending on context
dingolay	a dance movement
divvy up	share out
doan (have no sharp edge)	don't
doan (believe)	don't
donkey cart design	In the past an elaborately designed cart drawn by a donkey
don't wuk	do not work
door-mout	door entrance
doos	A do is a sort of street fete known as bashments in Jamaica. Kadooment is the ultimate do
douglah	part African, part Indian
drunking	very very drunk
duh fadda (money)	father
Easter trash-bone kite	Easter is kite flying season. A trash bone kite is a kite made of newspaper using the dried peel of the sugar cane to form a T on a piece of newspaper or brown paper, Cord is added to form the loops and a piece of stripped cloth

is added at the bottom to form a tail

ent gine	not going
ent just talking	not just talking
fight fuh de coocoo stick	When the sun shining and the rain falling, legend has it that the devil and his wife fighting to get control of the coocoo stick
force-ripeness	Forcing maturity e.g. fruit or young girls or boys who try to be adults
fowl-cock's tongue	Male fowl whose tongue usually has a >pip,' a hard scaly covering that has to be removed with ashes
frays	A small fish that is found in large shoals
frighten fuh dey shadow	Jittery fear
gaulins	Vulture, john crow, cubba
gine (to the theatre)	Going
ground-dirt	Fine dry dirt
guard-wall	A stone fence
guinea-grass	A grass used for feeding cattle
guttaperks	Slingshots
gypsy	fast, malicious, nosy
hamcutter	Ham sandwich served on a salt bread (a type of french roll) with pepper sauce
have a beef with	A problem, a quarrel

horsenicker	A hard grey seed that when rubbed gets very very hot
john crows	vultures
juk	Stick, poke, move, jerk
Kadooment Day	Last day of Crop Over Festival when costume bands parade on the streets of Barbados
kaiso	Another name for calypso
King Dyall	The name of a Bajan character who gave himself the name King when as a boy he realized that his contemporaries used to call all the white boys mister after he beat them in the swimming contests swimming out to Pelican Island and back. He said Acall me King or doan call me at all.@ He was an avid cricket fan who supported England at all times. He was always sartorially outfitted in colourful suits. He was of course a monarchist. An excellent domino player.
kitties	A shallow two sided drum with a snare attached used in a Bumbatuk band
kuss-kuss (grass)	A grass used in hedge rows of cane fields and whose aromatic roots are used to keep insects away from clothes. Also used to make perfume
laff	laugh
lahay	a dance movement
limers/lymers	People who lime, pass time in a public place with or without a purpose

lyming	A social activity of doing nothing while doing anything in a public place
leggo yuh hand at a rum shop	Spend money
log drum	A drum made from a tree body
long-side	As opposed to short side
loved his waters	A lover and consumer of rum
maguffey	A big man politically and/or socially
mannish-water	A soup made from the gonads and intestines of a male goat
manchineel	A poisonous evergreen tree found on the beaches of the Caribbean. Also known as manzanilla
Massa	Master, boss
mauby	a cool bitter frothy refreshing drink made from the bark of the mauby tree. Mauby bark usually comes from Guyana or Haiti. Unsweetened it is used medicinally.
mauga	emaciated, looking starve out
mek some sport	have fun
moola	Money
moses	A small in shore row boat
Mout	Mouth
mudda	Mother
mudda fiddle	Bass viol
nail-jooks	Puncture by nails usually in the foot

nigger yard	The area where enslaved or freed Africans lived on the plantation
nuff nuff clothes	A lot of clothes
nyam	An African word meaning eat but still used thruout the Caribbean
ole	Old
paling(s)	A fence usually made of metal sheeting, new or old or old flattened metal drums
pangola (grass)	An imported pasture grass used for feeding animals
pan yard	The rehearsal home of a steelband
passover	a light or heavy rainfall that is blown away by prevailing winds. Usually blue skies can be seen in the East confirming that the condition is a passover.
pawee mangoes	A tiny sweet mango not usually prized by people
pickney	A child.
Pompasetters	posers and pretenders
pon	On, upon
pond grass	A grass usually found growing around ponds. A runner, it is used to feed rabbits and other small stock
poo-poo	Insignificant
pooh-pooh	Ridicule
pope's nose	the fleshy part of a chicken or bird that holds the features

poxy-ness	Skin damaged by pock marks because of a pox
rab lands	Land with little or no top soil and useless for general crops
rockstones	Small stones capable of being used as missiles
Rotor rooter	Commercial name for a plumbers cleaning system
rum-shop	a bar or combination of a grocery shop with a bar at the side
Sankeys	Religious songs published by I D Sankey (1840-1908) and used in non-conformist churches in Caribbean (Allsopp)
scratch grain	a type of feed that is strewn on the ground for yard fowls to eat but which causes them to go thru the act of scratching the ground with their feet to get at the good grains
scotch	A little room made at the end of a bench on which others are seated to barely permit one more person to sit.@ (Allsopp)
scotched up	To squeeze, wedge or be wedged in!
Seine boats	a large shallow row boat that can carry about 20 men with a huge net which is partially placed in the water. Swimmers then chase schools of fish into the area blocked by the net and then the other sides are lowered. The net is then hauled by the seine boat to the nearest beach where the fish are then removed.
Service-a-songs	An evening of religious music and spoken performances usually held in a back yard or a community centre with lots of food and drink

shaggas	a type of crab that lives in the foreshore and hides in sprigs of moss. Likes to hold on to swimmers toes.
Shookster	a barrel stave with a wire on it that is used as a musical instrument by pressing it up against a chattel (wooden) house using the house as a resonator
sliver of wallaba	A long thin piece of wood broken off from wallaba wood, a reddish-brown wood from Guyana that is used for building and as fence posts especially in Barbados
smut lamps	A bottle filled with some type of flammable oil with a piece of rag as a wick. A type of flambeau.
sno-cones	Shaved iced covered with a variety a flavoured syrups
so so	OK. Nothing spectacular
soucouyan	An old woman of legend who sheds her skin which she hides then travels around at night as a ball of fire. She looks for people but especially babies so she can suck their blood and return to her skin before sun-up. The only way to get rid of her is find her skin and sprinkle it with salt and pepper or sprinkle rice grains around your house which she must pick-up and count before she could enter. Also know as old-higue, fire-hag and old-suck across the Caribbean
sour grass	A wild grass sometimes found growing on rab lands. Not a good fodder for animals for

harbours the grass canary in Barbados

stick-licker who used to pelt bois	The sport of stick-fighting. The wooden stick is called bois in the former French speaking islands.
stump-toes	Toes that are inadvertently struck on rocks and stones. Also a euphemisms for getting a clap
Susu	A co-operative savings system inherited from Africa. Also known as pardner in Jamaica, meeting turn in Barbados, box in Guyana and syndicate in Belize
swank	A cooling drink made of syrup or molasses, lime and water
tamarind season	In the post emancipation period, very few persons of African ancestry were employed during the out-of-crop period which was known as hard times or tamarind season where green tamarinds were eaten because of the shortage of food.
Tea meetings	A secular service of song with lots a speechifying using invented and meaningless big words and lots of a Latin phases. Usually chaired by a specialist wordsman.
tek care	Take care
The three Rs	W)Riting, Reading and (A)Rithmatic
third gang	During slavery and post emancipation period, children were organized in gangs known as the third gang to pick pond-grass and other

	Ameat@ for the animals on the plantation
tief	Thief
turn-collar	Reverends, priests, clergy
turpentine mangoes	A mango with an aftertaste flavour of turpentine
two-by-four ground	Small and insignificant
two-by-four lot	Small and insignificant
um	it
very (important)	Most important
vex	Angry
vodun	the popular religion of Haiti known as voodoo
wall houses	Houses made of softstone (coral stone or cement blocks
warri	An African mathematical game brought by Africans to the Caribbean and still played around the Caribbean
wash-pan	a large tub made out of galvanized iron
wheel and come again	Start again, repeat. A dance movement
woogala	plenty
wuking up	dancing with emphasis on the hips
wunna	Everybody
wutless	Worthless with a sense of wickedness, vulgarity and depravity

Index

Made in the USA
Monee, IL
21 August 2023

41388014R00204